SCREW FINDING YOUR PASSION

It's Within You, Let's Unlock it

Live with passion!

luz   a.k.a. Happyologist ☺

Susanna Halonen

Contents

Acknowledgements

The gratitude and thanks I feel to the people who have helped make this book happen is simply not possible to express in words. Funnily enough, as an author, I am left speechless – or should I say I am left *'wordless'*. However because of the amazing support, encouragement and inspiration I have received, I want to at least try.

First and foremost, I want to thank all the interviewees who agreed to take part in my research and share their amazing stories of passion. Without them, this book would be filled with empty pages. I also want to thank Dr Tim Lomas, who was my supervisor during my research on passion. He always found a way to calm my worries and stresses simply with his presence. He helped me discover the passionate way of being theory that this book is based on.

Next in line is my incredible support network all around me. Thank you to Mom and Dad for giving me unconditional love throughout my crazy adventures and for always encouraging me to aim high. Thank you to Hanna and Heidi, the two power ladies who are always the first to celebrate my successes with me and always ready to make me laugh when I'm feeling low. And thank you to my partner Elliot, who challenged me to write this book in the first place. In fact, it was in one of our first dates I told him that one day I wanted to write a book. His first response was, *"What are you waiting for?"* And that was the real beginning of my book. I also want to thank him for the little nudges of encouragement he gave me when I was needing them the most to keep going.

Other noteworthy mentions include one of my other professors, Dr Kate Hefferon, who was an inspiration to me in my positive psychology studies from day one. Her lecture on growth mindset opened up my eyes to a whole new world and has made me braver to take on new challenges to grow (like writing this book!). Thank you, Kate, for always showing what hard work is made of – and always doing it with great style (both metaphorically and literally!). Thank you also to Shawn Achor for being my introduction to positive psychology. It was your book, *The Happiness Advantage*, that led me into this magical world that eventually led to the discovery of this passion theory.

Last but not least, a massive thank you to all the Happyologist fans, followers and clients out there. Your support and encouragement has also played a huge role in making this book happen.

Introduction

Stop chasing your passion. Instead, look inwards and you will see that passion is right there, within you. So stop chasing it and start embracing it.

If you look around you, you'll notice that people have been engrained with the message that they must find their one and only passion. People have adopted the belief that in order to live a happy, fulfilling life, you must follow what you love, and build your whole life around doing what you love. Some say the only way to find happiness at work is to actually monetise what you love. These are all misconceptions offering a very limited view on passion that can actually work against your happiness, fulfilment and success. This book's aim is to shine light on a new, more opportunistic approach to passion, and help you unlock the passion within you, wherever you are.

When I was 18 years old, I followed exactly this misleading message of 'follow your passion' as I decided to study Equine and Business Management at a university in the middle of nowhere in western England. I had loved horses since the age of nine, and they had grown to be a big part of my daily life. I assumed that if I incorporated them into my studies, I would be able to build a life and career that I truly loved. I packed my bags, put my horse in the lorry, and drove across Europe from Sweden to England to get started on building this new dream life. I quickly realised how wrong I'd been to 'follow my passion'.

Within weeks of being at the secluded campus, which was full of young, hopeful riders, I started to feel lost, confused and alone. I realised it wasn't the world for me. I realised that I wanted horses to be a big part of my life, but I didn't want them to consume my life. They made my life whole, but I didn't want them to be my whole life. Doing horses 'full-time' killed the enjoyment I got from the sport and left me too exhausted to explore much else in life. After one semester at this university, I made the brave step to stop following my passion and re-direct my focus.

I transferred to a London university to study business and management, and moved my horse to a training stables in North London so I could still ride four to five times a week and compete actively. I was still able to do what I loved without being restricted in my career choices or exploring different pastime activities. This was my first personal experience that made me think twice about the 'follow your passion' message. Many more adventures in the years to come, both at university and shortly after at the start of my corporate career, made me realise that passion was a lot more complex than we make it out to be. And there were many more epiphanies around it, such as the one that came one and a half years into my corporate career.

I was six months away from finishing a prestigious European Graduate scheme in a big corporate, and I was trying to figure out what to do. I was sitting with a coach in a cafe in the hopes of finding some clarity through the session. Many who observed my confusion from the outside thought I was crazy to even think about shifting my career path. I was successfully climbing the career ladder, receiving lots of positive feedback and praise. I had an incredibly supportive partner, and a horse that I loved training after work and competing on weekends. Basically, life was good – yet I didn't feel it was fulfilling. I felt as if something was missing.

My coach challenged me with questions that forced me to be honest with myself. He asked anything from *"What do you actually want to do?"* to *"What would you do if you could do anything?"* to *"What makes your life worth living?"* In coaching, the coach always asks the client provocative questions to unlock their minds so they can tap into their subconscious and creativity. He was certainly doing that for me! And that's when I had my epiphany. I felt my life lacked passion. I felt I wasn't living a life true to me, and hence I was blocking the passion within me. And that's when I knew it was time for another big change.

This was the same time I discovered positive psychology through Shawn Achor's *The Happiness Advantage*.[1] It was an eye opener to the good side of psychology and I realised that's what I wanted to incorporate into my future career. Within 6 months of the coaching session I'd enrolled in positive psychology trainings, and within 12 months I'd been accepted to study a Master's of Science in Applied Positive Psychology in London. Things were on a roll. Within 12 months of the coaching session I also completed a coaching accreditation so I could start to help other people find clarity too. The powerful experience I had with my coach made me realise I wanted to help others to find the same sense of clarity my coach had helped me to discover.

In September 2012 I walked into my first positive psychology lecture – and I was over the moon. I was ready to go and change the world. I had never felt so right about anything. So when the opportunity came to choose what my scientific dissertation research would be on – the obvious choice was passion! And it's the revealing, surprising answers that came out of this research that led to the birth of this book.

Through my research I discovered the real secret to living life with passion: you have the power to unlock your passion at any point in time. You don't need to find the one thing you love, or obsess about religiously following what you love. Sometimes, as I've shown with my story (and others later on in the book), limiting your passion to one thing can make you feel sad rather than happy, deflated rather than energised, and more like a traitor rather than the real you. On the other hand, choosing to take control of your passion by learning to unlock it will help you live a life that makes you feel passionate, positive and proactive wherever you are.

This book has been split into three distinct parts that will motivate you to tap into your inner passion, learn how to activate it, and explore how to embed it into your life and career, starting today. The first part will introduce you to what passion is and why it's important, while highlighting the philosophical origins of passion as well as the scientific research behind it. The second part will feature the five keys to unlocking your passion,[2] with each of the keys explored in detail through inspirational stories, scientific research, and practical exercises to help you get started. The last part of the book will encourage you to take your passion everywhere you go, from the workplace to your relationship to life in general.

If you're excited to unlock the positive, powerful passion that lies inside of you, I encourage you to turn the page and join the passion journey where you're in control. Whichever way the journey takes you and however you wish to embark on it, there's no doubt it will leave you with a sense of energy, freedom and joy.

PART I:

PASSION IN LIFE

one

Exploring Passion

My mission in life is not merely to survive, but to thrive; and to do so with some passion, some compassion, some humour, and some style.
~ Maya Angelou ~

Passion is a form of positive energy that sits inside of you. It is something that you can choose to unlock from within you, and bring it out at any time. It's something that goes beyond motivation, and something that truly energises you on a whole different level. This doesn't mean that it has to be one activity, thing or person that brings out the passion in you, but instead you can choose to live your whole life with passion by pursuing the passionate way of being. This is how you stop chasing what you love but instead learn to find the love in what you do.

Stop Looking for Your Passion
There is this misconception in society that in order to be happy you need to follow your passion. If you don't

know what your one and only passion is, you need to go and find it. People have been engrained with the message that you can only have one true passion, and that you must build your whole life around it if you want to be happy, fulfilled and successful. This view is very limiting and dangerous for many reasons.

First of all, what if you don't know what your passion is? What if you've adopted this belief and are desperate to find your one and only passion? This could easily lead you into a state of despair, endless procrastination and lack of action because you're afraid of doing anything unrelated to this 'one passion' you have yet to discover. It can make you feel as if you have no control over your life, over your passion and over your happiness. This is a recipe for disaster. If you believe that you have no control, you lose your sense of autonomy and hence are not motivated to do what needs to be done in order to unlock your passion and happiness.

Or maybe you have a very clear idea of what you love to do but you don't want to build your whole life around this one activity. Maybe you know, just as I experienced, that trying to make one activity you love 'your everything' can actually kill the love for it. It can kill your enjoyment of it as you start to see it more like work and something you have to do. Again, it can take the whole sense of control out of the picture again.

It could even be that you know what you love to do, but you simply don't have the resources to build your life around it. Maybe you're limited physically, geographically, financially or time-wise in terms of pursuing this one thing you love. This can also be very deflating and demotivating. And it really doesn't have to be that way. There's no need to tie your passion, enjoyment and happiness to one thing.

Even if you were able to build your whole life around this one love, imagine how you would feel if you realised it didn't bring you the happiness and fulfilment you were looking for. Research has even supported this notion with the concept of obsessive passion; you are so consumed by this one activity that you neglect other areas of your life, such as your own mental and physical wellbeing. It can have a very negative effect on your life and your happiness overall. How would you feel then? There might be a sense of panic there, and I definitely can admit to feeling that when I realised the horse university wasn't for me. I was very confused and distraught. Was this really my one shot at happiness? Since this didn't work out, is it all doom and gloom now? Well I'm here to tell you that's certainly not the case! You have the power to unlock your passion, and with it your happiness and fulfilment, by taking a more proactive approach towards it.

Then there's also the concept of loving many things. Many coaching clients have come to me asking for direction because they feel they are passionate about many things. They feel even more overwhelmed and confused, and again their life is dangerously full of indecision paralysis because they're so afraid of 'following' the wrong passion. I have helped them understand, just like I will help you understand through this book, that passion is a way of being, a way of life and a positive energy source within you that you can tap into at any time. There's no need to limit yourself to one pursuit and call that your passion.

Now I'm not advocating to never do things you love or things you enjoy. Of course you should do the activities that bring you joy and excitement. That's exactly why I've kept the horses in my life and still train and compete very actively. They bring me an immense sense of joy, achievement and many other things! But the one thing I am asking you to reconsider is the idea that the only way to find happiness, fulfilment and success is to build your whole life around following 'your one true passion'. Let's face it, as humans we are continuously evolving and changing, as are our lives. So the idea of having one passion is quite daunting and in a way unrealistic. Are you going to commit your lifetime to one thing?

I'm sure you can already start to see that the 'follow your passion' or 'find your passion' formula isn't as straightforward as people make it sound. It has many complications to it and it can actually work against you building a happy, fulfilling life. In the worst case scenario, it can make you freeze with inaction and wait for things to happen. And it's especially then that it becomes dangerous because in essence you're waiting to live your life. You're waiting for someone or something else to bring your life to you. I urge you to stop waiting and take control. Take control of your passion so you can take a more proactive approach to it. Take control so you can live a passionate life that's more likely to lead to real happiness and fulfilment. Take control by pursuing a passionate way of being and embracing the positive passion energy throughout your whole life.

Origins of Passion

Even philosophical viewpoints of passion that arose hundreds and thousands of years ago introduced this all-encompassing perspective on passion. It's a perspective that makes you more motivated to take control of that inner positive energy within you because it's clear that if you're proactive you can truly unlock its power. But before we dive into unlocking that passion within you, let's explore the role philosophy has in shaping the current misconception around passion – that you need to 'find your passion' and 'follow your passion'. In fact, it's quite ironic how it was already Aristotle who presented this more opportunistic, all-encompassing perspective on passion, and how the philosophers who followed have actually polluted the passion perspective that was the most encouraging and powerful one after all.

Passion has received both a positive and negative light in philosophy in the past. The word *'passion'* itself originates from the Latin word *'passio'*, which means suffering[3] – so not a very positive start for passion! But it was already in Aristotelian times that passion got introduced in the positive light that it is seen today. Passion was seen as an element of *eudaimonia*, which basically meant you identified with your true self and lived your life in harmony with your true self.[4]

Already then, passion was seen as something that shone when you were being the real you and expressing yourself authentically. Aristotle philosophised on how living life as your true self enabled your greatest fulfilment and made it possible for you to reach your highest potential. Similarly today, in the field of positive psychology, *eudaimonia* refers to a type of happiness that occurs when you express your true spirit and do things that are worth doing.[5] In other words, when you're being the real you your passion comes out and when you're contributing to the greater good you find a meaningful sense of happiness.

Since Aristotle, the philosophical debate on passion has continued through numerous centuries. In the early 17th century, René Descartes introduced the view that tied passion and reason together.[6] He believed passion drove strong positive emotions, such as joy and awe, as long as reason was also in the picture. He believed that reason had to accompany the powerful passion energy in order to ensure the individual remained in control. He spoke of reason coming from the mind, which controls the body, but also spoke of how the body, from where he believed passion came, could influence the mind.

Later in the same century, Baruch Spinoza argued that unwelcome thoughts, thoughts that were negative or caused human suffering, were driven by the uncontrollable power of one's passion.[7] He believed people who fully embraced the passion within them were slaves to it with no control and hence suffered through it. Here you can already see the link to today's psychological concept of obsessive passion in which one passion consumes you in a negative way. Baruch Spinoza saw passion as something that drove an uncontrollable evil, whereas he saw reason as something that drove acceptable thoughts.

The 19th century brought Georg Wilhelm Friedrich Hegel's determined view that passion was essential if you wanted to reach your highest level of achievement.[8] He believed passion was the key driver in you being able to fulfil your utmost potential. This was followed by existentialists Søren Kierkegaard and Friedrich Nietzsche, who saw passion as something that drove you to do anything.[9] Søren Kierkegaard claimed that life without passion is a deficient life with no energy, no drive and a limited experience of emotions. He believed the only way to live a fulfilling life was to push your passion to its limits as only then would you be able to achieve the impossible in life. He said that if passion was present in your life, then you would be able to make decisions that were driven by the real self.

Friedrich Nietzsche advanced Hegel's view of *"Nothing great has been achieved without passion"*, to *"Nothing at all has been achieved without passion"*.[10] Nietzsche saw passion as the power that dominated a person if reason was not acknowledged, and hence raised the same concern René Descartes did two centuries earlier: passion had its dangers if let loose. Saying that, he also argued that denying your passion from coming out would be denying life itself and the meaning that could come from expressing your passion.

These philosophical viewpoints already show the different perspectives that have led to the conversations we have today on how we deal with passion, and whether it benefits us or puts us at risk. The philosophers across different centuries spoke of the importance of passion in living a fulfilling life, yet they never argued passion had to be tied to one activity or thing. Hence it's somewhat unclear how the 'find your passion' and 'follow your passion' messages have become so popularised and where they actually came from. We can go as far back as Aristotelian times to see this wasn't the message that started the passion conversations – in fact, it was quite the opposite. Aristotle saw passion as a form of energy that was within an individual.

Passion in Psychological Research

These conversations have led to passion being explored from a scientific angle too. Passion has been incredibly under-researched in the field of psychology (or any scientific field for that matter!), and what little has been researched is quite limiting. It was Canadian professor Dr Robert J. Vallerand who put passion on the map in the early 2000s alongside the rise of positive psychology. Positive psychology focuses on optimal human functioning, what makes life worth living, and how to help individuals, organisations and communities to thrive. Dr Vallerand introduced the idea that passion is one of the key components that make life worth living,[11] and has been researching the idea ever since.

Dr Vallerand took a different angle to his passion research than was originally suggested by Aristotle. He focused his research on how an individual ties his passion to a particular activity rather than acknowledging passion as something all-encompassing that runs throughout life. Passion, in his eyes, is defined as an activity one enjoys, finds important, and invests time and energy doing. He touches on the philosophical idea of passion being a part of the true self by taking the standpoint that the passion towards an activity is something that becomes internalised in one's identity.

Similar to what was already suggested in the philosophical origins of passion, Dr Vallerand also presents a positive and negative side to this passion one feels towards an activity. In fact, he distinguished two different types of passion which have two different types of consequences. He introduced the idea of a harmonious passion and an obsessive passion towards an activity.[12] Harmonious passion is developed and internalised into one's identity by choice, and it's accompanied by flexible persistence. This means you choose to pursue the activity for the sake of enjoyment and you are able to do that without causing any harm to your other life domains.

Obsessive passion, as the name itself suggests, leads to an inflexible persistence in the activity and it often leads to harmful consequences in other life domains because there is no real sense of balance. This is the type of uncontrollable passion that Baruch Spinoza philosophised about. Even though Dr Vallerand discovered that people still identified with the activity even when they were obsessively passionate about it, they found that their choice to pursue the activity was driven by both internal and external pressures. For example, ballet dancers with obsessive passion for ballet dance were driven to train endlessly in order to be accepted by their peers and in order to intrinsically feel they were trying hard enough. Their self-esteem was dependent on the success of this obsessive passion. This resulted in them training even through injury and against doctor's recommendations, which led to long-term negative consequences.

These two different types of passion have been explored by Dr Vallerand and other psychologists in different settings, and the findings have consistently linked harmonious passion to happiness and higher levels of performance.[13] Obsessive passion on the other hand has not been associated with either, except in elite sports. One study that looked at elite ice-hockey players in Canada showed that obsessive passion was tied to higher levels of performance because that elite sporting environment demanded a near 'obsessive' commitment to the sport in order to be able to excel.[14] Again, here you can see the dangers of tying your passion to one activity as it has the risk of becoming obsessive and taking over your life. So instead of living a life with all-encompassing passion, you end up living a life swallowed up by one passion. This is very limiting and can quickly become very dangerous as your whole life, and ultimately your happiness and sense of achievement, depend on the success of this one activity.

Researching Passion

I found this view on passion very limiting, especially after my own challenging passion journeys. This is why

I decided to explore passion further in my research. I wanted to see what people actually had to say about passion. I wanted to discover if what Aristotle and the other philosophers spoke about had some scientific truth in them. This is when I embarked on another passion adventure myself. For the 12 months that I had to complete my Master's of Science in Applied Positive Psychology, I immersed myself in anything and everything to do with passion. And that's when I decided to research passion through my science-based Master's thesis.

Because the existing research on passion (before my research) had been based purely on quantitative studies – that is, studies based on people answering different types of scales by rating themselves – I wanted to explore passion on a deeper level. I wanted to talk to people. I wanted to hear what people had to say when I asked them what passion means to them. I wanted to explore passion more deeply than some numbers on a scale. I wanted to give passion a real voice. And it is through this research that I saw, for the first time, how limiting the existing messaging around 'following your passion' is. It is through this research that I realised we all have the power to tap into the positive passion energy that lies within us.

For my research, I wanted to find individuals to interview who were high in energy and passionate about spreading their message. Hence the obvious choice was to talk to people who identified themselves as being very passionate. Immediately it was TEDx speakers who came to mind. These are individuals who have spoken about a message they are passionate about in a local

TEDx conference. These conferences sit under the TED umbrella, a non-profit organisation devoted to spreading ideas around innovation, collaboration and progress.[15] And so my real exploration began!

The interviews I conducted were kept very open as I wanted to truly discover what they had to say about passion, rather than spoon feed them with any concrete ideas. And boy am I glad I kept it open – what I discovered was truly eye-opening! This research made it clear that these individuals didn't tie their passion to one activity or one thing – they lived their whole lives with passion. They chose to use passion to find a sense of energy, freedom and happiness, rather than letting it limit them. They chose to find love in what they did, rather than run after what they loved. They chose to pursue the passionate way of being.

Passionate Way of Being

As Jane* described to me in her interview, *"Passion feels like it ought to be something that runs through you, and through your life, and it's integral to your identity"* (*names have been changed to protect the anonymity of the interview participants). She saw passion as something which was inseparable from her and ran across her life. This is exactly what pursuing the passionate way of being is all about: the passion is in you as the individual, rather than in a specific activity you do.[16] This makes it possible for you to direct your passion to many things in your life, opening a whole world of opportunities to you. It enables you to choose passion as a way of being, rather than passion being a positive attitude towards a particular activity.

This brings forth the question of control and proactivity again, as Fred* pointed out in his interview:

Do you do what you love or does what you love do you? Umm ... I don't know ... I think when it comes to the human instrument, you know, there's the instrument and there's the music. And I don't know if the music comes to the instrument or if the instrument generates the music. I think somewhere in between those two things is the actual reality of what it is when you see a human doing what they love.

It's this 'human instrument' which holds the passion inside of you. It's this human instrument that you have the power to control so you can generate your own music. When Fred refers to the 'in between', he speaks of the positive passion energy which creates a self-sustaining spiral in your life and throughout your activities when you learn to unlock it and keep control of it. The more you learn to unlock your passion, the more natural it becomes to you, and the more your passion starts to reinforce itself throughout your life.

This type of all-encompassing passion leads to overall happiness, a sense of energy and a sense of freedom. Because you learn to find love in what you do, you learn to find the good and appreciate things from a completely new angle. This all in turn will further light the fire within you. The happiness it brings is also on many levels. It helps you experience more positive emotions, such as joy, excitement, awe, hope, inspiration and pride. It makes you feel good and boosts the production of those happy hormones, also known as endorphins, in your brain. It also gives you a sense of meaning, because finding love in what you do means you find the purpose behind the activities in your life. This is also one of the keys to unlocking your passion, which are discussed in more detail in Chapter Four.

When you learn to harness this passionate way of being through the five keys described in Part Two, passion becomes inseparable from you. Passion becomes a form of positive energy that you can embrace and use across all aspects of your life. Best of all, learning to harness it will only lead to more positive energy coming through it.

The five keys that unlock the passionate way of being ensure that you live a life that's authentic, purposeful and fulfilling. Each of the keys has a different way of unlocking the positive passion energy within you, and they are all discussed in turn in Part Two. But let me start by introducing them to you, first visually and then descriptively.

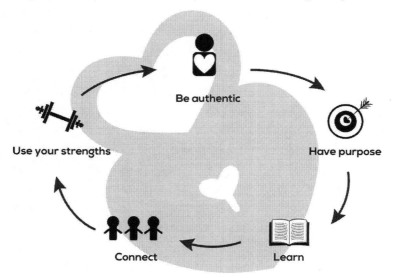

1. Be the Authentic You

Just as philosophy suggested hundreds and thousands of years ago, the key ingredient to unlocking your passion is to be your true self. It's about understanding, and perhaps discovering, who is the authentic you. It's about becoming more self-aware so you understand what is important to you, what fuels you and what is the foundation of your true identity. When you are able to discover your true self, and what you stand for, you're much more likely to live a life that's aligned with your values and beliefs. And it's this authenticity, this honesty and self-compassion towards yourself, that lights the fire within you and unlocks the positive passion energy.

One of the foundations of authenticity is understanding what your values and beliefs are. Your personal values are the virtues you live your life by. These are the qualities that you see as admirable and good. These are the things you base your decisions on. Your beliefs also have a big role in your identity, influencing the life you build and the opinions you have. When you align your behaviour with your values and beliefs, and create a sense of awareness to do this proactively, you are able to ignite the type of positive energy that fuels your passion and fulfilment.

In Chapter Three you'll be able to explore what your values and beliefs are, and how they actually shape your decisions. You'll be able to reflect on whether you believe you are living your life as the authentic you, and how you can bring more of your real self out.

2. Understand Your Why

Another key ingredient that unlocks your passion within is understanding your why. What is your purpose in life right now? What is the kind of positive impact you're looking to create? Be brave about exploring the motivational drivers behind your actions. Think about what makes you get out of bed in the morning, and what brings you excitement and inspiration. Find a purpose that's meaningful to you, not simply something that's been branded as 'acceptable' by your friends, family or society. This purpose links back to the whole sense of authenticity as you need to find a purpose that you connect with through your values and beliefs.

It's this purpose which helps you understand the kind of positive impact you want to create – and acknowledge the positive impact you are *already* creating. Connecting with this purpose sends a more spiritual passion energy through you as you understand your role in the world. You see the bigger picture and you're able to shift your perspective to one that appreciates the unique role you have in making the world progress. It gives you a sense of meaning which further enhances the desire to create positive impact.

A big part of understanding your why is about acknowledging that life is dynamic, and that this why may shift over time. But if you check in with it regularly, and remain aware of it, you continue to live a life that's authentic to you and one that keeps creating positive impact in new ways. These elements will all be explored in Chapter Four where you'll be able to ask yourself questions that will help you understand your why.

3. Master the Art of Learning

The third passion principle is truly embracing the learning and growth journey you are continuously on in life. When you find new ways to develop and grow, both in your daily life and in your career, you ignite a sense of excitement and adventure which fuels the passion energy within you. It also makes you more likely to spot opportunities and take up challenges in order to grow.

When you're learning you're at your happiest. You get a sense of fulfilment and accomplishment. You get to develop and grow. You get to embark on an exciting adventure of unknowns where you have to overcome challenges and go out of your comfort zone. You have to tap into your courage and bravery, and persevere despite the fears you feel. It's this unknown and the curiosity to explore it that helps you tap into the passion that lights up when you're pushing yourself the most. It's also the path to mastery, and truly embracing the ability to master a skill, trait or particular activity you enjoy will keep the fire inside you burning strong.

But most importantly, it's about mastering the art of learning itself. It's about understanding how every minute, every environment, every person you encounter, and every situation is an opportunity for you to learn. You can learn about yourself, about others, and about life overall. Don't limit your learning to one particular thing but truly embrace it wherever you are. In Chapter Five I'll ask you to re-visit how you see learning and provoke you to come up with new, creative ways on how you can master your learning journey.

4. Connect with Your Tribe

Human beings are social creatures. Just like many herd animals, we thrive through social connection, and relationships are a big part of our lives. And it is the right connections which light the fire inside of us (both romantically and non-romantically!). Your tribe includes the people who inspire you, encourage you and motivate you to keep going. They are your steady rock in times of challenge, and your energising rocket fuel when the going is good. You are very similar to them, helping them keep their fire alive. You keep each other going.

These connections could be anyone – from your friends to your colleagues to your family to your clients. Maybe it's someone you met only once at a chance encounter, but they left something with you which helps you keep your fire alive. Maybe it's an idol you met once or interact with through social media, and what they do inspires you to keep doing what you do best. Maybe it's your trainer or your coach or the people in your network who do similar work to what you do.

Whoever they are, they connect with you in a way that makes you feel confident in who you are, helps you believe in what you do and encourages you to keep working hard even in the face of challenge. In Chapter Six you will get a chance to remind yourself of who your tribe is, how you connect with it, and find new people to join your tribe if the desire is there.

5. Play with Your Strengths

In today's society we are often reminded of our weaknesses – be it through the way media portrays what is 'beautiful', what society expects you to have achieved by the age of 30, or how organisations focus on your weaknesses in your yearly performance reviews. These approaches are backwards and make us more miserable, less productive and less motivated than ever before. It's time you learned to embrace your strengths and put them to good use.

Research has repeatedly shown how being able to use your strengths (at work and in life) makes your days more enjoyable, boosts your productivity and performance, and also improves your overall happiness levels. Believing in these natural skill sets you have and using them in different ways also help you to tap into the positive passion energy within you. The key here, again, is to use them in different ways rather than tying them to one thing. It's the variety that adds the spice to your life and helps you make the most of your strengths, while expanding the positive impact you create to new spheres.

Chapter Seven will help you to explore your strengths, become more aware of them, and come up with new ideas for how you can use them more to your benefit – as well as to the benefit of those around you. The more self-aware you become, the more able you will be to maximise your talents, and the easier it will become to use these strengths to generate the positive impact you're looking to create.

It's Your Turn

This book is designed to help you unlock the positive passion energy within you so you can live a fulfilling life that's true to you. I want you to be free from the limitations that 'find your passion' and 'follow your passion' impose on you. I want you to feel the way I did when I realised I could choose to pursue a passionate way of being. I hope you'll enjoy the passion journey that you'll embark on throughout this book, and long after it as you learn to live your whole life with passion. After all, what's life without passion? Now I ask you to put your warrior gear on and take the first step on this journey.

> *A warrior does not give up what he loves,*
> *he finds the love in what he does.*
> ~ Socrates ~

two

Why is Passion Important

*Nothing great in the world has ever been
accomplished without passion.*
~ Georg Wilhelm Friedrich Hegel ~

Life without passion is a life not fully lived. It is a life
lived without expressing your utmost potential. It is a
life lived without colour. Imagine getting up every day,
going through your same routine before work, at work
and after work without any real excitement in your day.
Life would be really dull, and in a way quite 'grey' or
'beige'. What passion does is that it adds colour to your
life. Imagine jumping out of bed every day with excitement, anticipating the great adventures that the day will
bring. When you learn to tap into your inner passion,
bring it out and take control of it, you'll learn to bring
more excitement and fun into your everyday, be it at
work or in life.

The people I interviewed spoke about how living a
life with passion gave them a sense of happiness, freedom and energy. Overall, it enhanced their lives on

so many levels. The more they lived life with passion, the more they felt the passion come out, feeling a reinforcing, self-sustaining passion spiral happening within them and throughout their life. They also spoke of how it affected their motivation, and went further than engaging them in their life, and how this tied to them being more persistent in their pursuits. It even broadened their perspective on life, helping them appreciate what they had and encouraging them to create positive impact. Passion was their secret weapon for living a successful, fulfilling life.

Passion and Happiness
Similar to the original philosophical ideas on passion, recent psychological research has linked passion to happiness on many levels. Passion makes you feel good, helps you experience more positive emotions and gives you a sense of purpose. It makes you feel more satisfied with your life, which in turn makes you more proactive in making decisions that further boost your positive emotions. In psychological terms, it feeds both your hedonic and eudaimonic happiness.[17]

Hedonic happiness refers to you experiencing positive emotions, such as joy and pleasure, and being satisfied with life. It's associated with *subjective wellbeing* which encompasses experiencing more positive emotions and moods than negative ones, and being more satisfied than dissatisfied with your life.[18] When you learn to bring your passion out, you learn to experience more of the positive emotions and moods throughout your day, rather than purely through one activity or one thing. With passion you learn to appreciate the good in many things and hence find more enjoyment through a variety of activities.

Eudaimonic happiness on the other hand refers to a sense of meaning that you experience from your life which gives you a sense of fulfilment.[19] In essence, you feel your life is worthwhile as it is full of purpose, challenges and growth. When you learn to pursue a passionate way of being, you tap into your inner passion and the clarity of purpose that comes from it. You become clearer about your bigger purpose and your why, and the kind of positive impact you want to create. The magic of the passion is also self-reinforcing on this level, increasing your desire to create more positive impact the more you do it.

Pursuing this passionate way of being helps you build a very fulfilling and engaging life driven by the enjoyment you find in doing things that are aligned with your true self. It gives you a sense of experience that what you're doing is worthwhile, and helps you focus on your purpose (discussed in depth in Chapter Four). It's this happiness that also helps you connect with people on a new level, shifting the mirror neurones in your brain into a setting that helps you relate to others through positive emotions. It also exerts a type of continuity and consistency in your life that is naturally very dynamic, letting your passion encourage you to consistently choose happiness on a daily basis.

Passion and Freedom
Choosing to pursue a passionate way of being over focusing your passion on one activity or pursuit will make you

feel free.[20] You will be able to tap into more opportunities as you'll feel as if you have more choice, options, and opportunities throughout your life. Unlike a passion that's tied to one thing, you won't feel boxed in, caged or limited in how you live your life. You will feel as if there are no borders to your creativity and adventures, and that you can in fact fly high in whichever direction you decide to go. You feel as if anything is possible. One of the interviewees in my research described this effect beautifully:

> *Really anything is possible. In many ways that's why I love my passion so much, because I feel that it's so flexible, and it's so open.*

Some refer to this sense of freedom "*almost like a spiritual experience*". When you are able to tap into your passion consistently, and the freedom that comes with it, you will feel safer in a world that's full of risks. You'll connect with yourself and with the world in a new kind of way. As you'll discover in Chapter Three and Chapter Four, this connectedness to yourself and the world ties in with living your life as your authentic self, producing the positive impact you're looking to create. It's this alignment with your true self that not only brings out your passion but gives you an unrestricted freedom to pursue things important to you. One interviewee in my research described living life with passion as something that brought her into alignment with her true self: "*I come face to face with my value. I'm free*".

Another one spoke about how getting in touch with the positive passion energy within them was a *"freeing experience"* that helped them realise *"the reality of who I am."* This reality of who you are, which can also be referred to as authenticity, is one of the key elements that unlocks your passion, and then is further enhanced by your passion once it's out (this is discussed in detail in Chapter Three). It's about accepting who you are, and embracing it, as well as acknowledging the change that you go through throughout your life. It's this sense of freedom that comes alongside passion that makes change easier to face and use in a positive manner. All these elements of freedom are tied to the energising effect unlocking your passion also has on you.

Passion and Energy
All life is a form of energy, and hence without energy there is no life. Passion feeds a spiritual type of energy that makes you feel more engaged and driven in your various pursuits.[21] Unlocking your passion within leads you into unlocking a positive energy spiral that sustains itself. It means that you're not only investing energy into doing things, but you're actually getting energised in return. This energy will further reinforce the real you and give you the strength to be authentic throughout your life. This is what will help you realise how passion is the power of positive spiritual energy.

After a busy, productive day you might feel physically tired but spiritually energised. You'll realise that living a life with passion re-energises you in a new kind of way, refuelling you so you can keep going. It gives you a child-like energy that makes you immersed in curiosity, inspiration and wonder. You'll be able to spot, and appreciate, the beauty in the world and experience more wow. You'll become more enthusiastic about new things and remember to bring in the fun.

Pursuing this passionate way of being throughout your life makes you very engaged, absorbed and excited by the things you do. The more alignment you're able to spot between your authentic self and what you do, the more immersed you'll become in what you do. This in turn will feed your positive passion energy further and add to this self-sustaining buzzing vitality that you experience. Psychologists refer to this as *subjective vitality*. This is defined as something that helps you consciously realise you possess an incredibly powerful energy source within you, and that you have control over it. This makes you feel truly alive.

There is also a way for you to spread your positive passion energy around you, and just like most moods and emotions, it's very contagious. Not only are you refuelling your energy tank when you're living an authentic life and expressing your passion, but you're also helping others fuel theirs. Passion is a type of powerhouse for your energy levels, and that's why it also affects your performance.

Passion and Performance
When it comes to success, or more specifically performance in the workplace, passion has an important role

to play. With employees locked in ever increasing work-loads today, it's even more important to make sure the passion is there so they can take a more positive and pro-active approach to their work. When employees choose to engage in their work passionately, they will learn to work smarter not harder. They will be able to see the positive in times of challenge, and hence they'll be able to think more creatively at those times. This is especially important because we naturally have a negativity bias within us.

We are naturally more focused on the negative and have to work against our evolutionary background to make positivity a habit.[22] Before, we needed the nega-tivity to survive as it alerted our fight, flight or freeze response when we were faced with real physical threats in our environment. Negativity blocks our creativity as it draws our entire attention on the threat, challenge or whatever it is that's got our negativity going. This was useful in the times when we had a lion chasing us and we needed our focus on that, but in today's work environ-ment it's incredibly counterproductive. If we now face a challenge or obstacle at work, the negativity bias auto-matically makes our brains obsess over that if we don't take control. The more we focus on that challenge, the more narrow-minded we become, which in turn pre-vents us from thinking more creatively to get out of the challenge.

We now need to re-train our brains so they are adept at performing at their best in today's world. And this is where passion comes in. Passion opens up our minds by combining elements of intrinsic motivation, positivity and the energy we hold within us, to make us much more proactive, creative and persistent when we work towards our goals. It gives us the confidence and courage to act to make the best out of everything. This in turn makes us much more positive which in turn makes us more likely to succeed.

Research has repeatedly shown that positivity is a key driver of performance.[23] When you're happy your brain releases a chemical called dopamine which activates all of the learning centres in your brain.[24] This means you immediately have more brain power to use! As a result, positive employees are more creative and innovative, more productive, more resilient in the face of stress, quicker to bounce back from failures, more effective in producing sales, and more likely to receive positive feedback from customers. One of the most famous studies demonstrating this was Alice Isen's work with doctors.[25] She found that when she induced positive emotions in doctors by giving them a bag of sweets before a diagnosis, the doctors were quicker and more accurate in their diagnosis of illnesses. How crazy is that!

Passion falls into the same bag with positivity as the two naturally reinforce each other. When you're positive you can more easily bring out your passion, and when you're passionate you're naturally more positive. Dr Vallerand's research on passion has repeatedly found that passion fuels performance because it enables you to make the most out of your strengths, it boosts your self-esteem, it encourages you to adapt your behaviour to situations, and it increases your wellbeing.[26] Basically it helps you find a sense of self-awareness which in turn creates an inner drive towards your goals, making you more motivated and productive.

This is especially important in today's workplaces when only 25% of your success is predicted by intelligence and technical skills. The remaining 75% of your success is dependent on your optimism, the belief that your behaviour matters, your social connections, and the way you perceive stress.[27] Understanding your inner passion and learning to unlock it helps you find more optimism, become more proactive with your behavioural choices, connect with the right people, and react to stress in a more constructive way. This is all connected to the outlook you choose to have on your life and in life in general.

Your Outlook on Your Life
When I left my corporate job to study for my Master's in something I truly cherished (positive psychology, that is!), I saw the world from a whole new angle. I started to allow myself to be the real me, and this is what started to really unlock my inner passion. I appreciated things I loved even more, I saw things which frustrated me from a new perspective, and I got this huge desire to be a part of something bigger. Pursuing the passionate way of being doesn't only lead to happiness, freedom and a sense of energy. It also leads to the desire to make a real difference. It gives you a new pair of eyes that brings

more compassion in, both towards yourself and towards others. It helps you connect with yourself on a deeper level, and with other people and their challenges in a unique way.

When you learn to bring out your passion you find you want to help others do the same. You want to share the happiness, freedom and energy you feel, and help them recreate that for themselves. You start to understand people you perhaps didn't understand before, and you realise that there is room for all kinds of unique characters in this world. Everyone, in their own unique ways, is working with a purpose in mind even if they may not fully realise it.

Living life with passion adds colour to your life. You'll experience life in High Definition or in 3D. You'll become more in tune with your five senses and use them to have more moving experiences. You'll find gratitude in things you never thought you would, and you'll appreciate challenges for what they are. You'll find a place where you can go to get this positive passion energy, and equally you'll recognise the peaceful quietness needed at times to recharge. Passion doesn't mean living life at full speed, but in living life fully.

Dangers of Passion
When you learn to unlock your passion, you'll recognise the powerful effect it has on you and your life. This is where you need to make sure you're in charge of the speed you're going and the direction you're heading in. Sometimes, passion can be too powerful. Existing

research on passion has already shown that if you direct your passion only to one activity or one thing, it can take over you and your life completely. This is what I introduced as obsessive passion in Chapter One. When you direct all your passion energy into one activity, there is a huge danger that you start to neglect other areas of your life, including your physical and mental wellbeing. This is why research has shown that it can also have a negative impact on your happiness.[28] In essence, you're putting all your eggs in one basket and your happiness is dictated by that basket alone. This sole focus on one basket alone is very risky.

However, if you choose to pursue the passionate way of being (with the five elements I outline in Part Two), you'll be less likely to enter an obsessive passion because you're not limiting passion to one activity. That means you are keeping control of your passion, rather than letting one activity take control of all of your passion. Saying that, passion is an incredibly powerful form of energy so it can overwhelm you, especially at the beginning of your journey and when you experience big successes. These feed the positive passion energy as if it was on steroids so it's important to stay aware of this.

The more in touch with your passion you become, the more a part of you it becomes. That can be scary at first because it does start to rule you a little bit. When it starts to rule you too much, and becomes overpowering, it can lead to challenges and conflicts if you feel like you have lost control. As much as your passion is expected to lead you as a form of energy, equally you need to lead it in the right direction. If you experience losing control, you can get stuck in a more negative spiral which will prevent you from proactively taking back control. This can happen if you feel your passion energy take over but you forget to keep it on track with your authentic self. You ought to remember your values and your why, and keep redirecting your passion back to them if it has got lost in the process.

One of the things that could lead to this loss of control is obsessing over goals. As I have already introduced the five passion keys, you know a key component of living life with passion is following a purpose and having some sort of positive impact. This gives you a sense of focus in your pursuits and it is very likely that it leads to you setting goals aligned with this focus. Goals are very useful as they remind you where you are heading and help you make decisions that help you move forward towards them. But it's when the focus for one specific goal becomes an obsession that it becomes an issue.

One of my interviewees referred to this as *"wanting so much that it does hurt"*. Someone else referred to this desire almost as an addiction, clearly voicing it by saying, *"I don't think I'm someone who follows what I love, I'm someone who's got addicted to something."* Here we can see the negativity that arises from this pressure to 'follow what you love' and how it's completely backfired in this person's life. Others spoke about getting on the hamster wheel to keep going, growing and reaching your goals, but never being able to get off. They spoke about setting a goal, working to achieve it, achieving it, and then quickly setting new goals to work towards. Unlocking your positive passion energy can set you into an obsessive goal spiral if you get hooked on the goal achievement and forget to keep them in alignment with who you are. This in turn led them to feeling like they wanted to escape.

Sometimes when the passion gets so strong and so blinding, it overwhelms you and you want to run away. Fred* felt this at one stage in his chosen career when he experienced such burnout that he saw an escape as the only way to overcome it. He moved me with his words as he said, *"I was so disillusioned and hurt by the whole thing, that I took an entire year off."* Personally, this really touched me because I realised I could truly relate to exactly what he was describing. Even though I never walked away from something to escape, I remember really wanting to a few times in my life. I could relate to the disillusion and hurt that he felt, as he was putting his heart and soul into his pursuits to the extent that he was wearing himself out.

Personally I've gone through that too – both with my Happyologist business and my competitive dressage riding with my horse. Those two pursuits are who I am and what I love, yet sometimes I give so much to them I forget to take care of me. And that's when I've felt the desire to escape, to run away, especially from the expectations I put on myself. However, I've also realised that sometimes when your passion is so strong in your life that you feel like you want to escape, that's actually a sign that you're heading in the right direction. This is often the key moment when you have to embrace the passion energy, take control of it, and use it positively in the right direction to move forward.

This is also what Fred* found. After escaping for a year, he quickly found his way back to his passionate way of being as he'd taken the time to understand how to manage it more effectively. He'd understood how to manage it by staying true to himself. After all, some of this desire to escape is founded in the fear of being true to yourself, and the fear of what other people around you think. Albert*, another interviewee, spoke about how living life with passion made him feel exposed: *"When, when I've explored my passions, and talked about them openly ... It lays you vulnerable to other people's prejudices and assumptions."* This is true. Living life with passion means being vulnerable because you're connecting with your true self, and you let the whole world see who you truly are. It takes courage to stick with the authentic you and keep pursuing the passionate way of being. But in the end, as I've already pointed out, it's well worth it.

These dangers of passion that I've spoken of here are related to the obsessive passion I already introduced. In one of the studies Dr Vallerand did with his colleagues, he found that an obsessive passion led to losing control of their excitement for the activity and obsessing over its accompanying goals.[29] In this particular study, the researchers discovered that dance students with an obsessive passion were more likely to continue dancing even in the face of injury because of their inability to let go of this one activity, even momentarily, to which they'd tied all their passion energy. This is similar to the stories I heard on goal obsession, and how in extreme cases they even led to depression and a complete sense of hopelessness.

As with most things in life that are worth having, passion also comes with two sides. It can be incredibly fulfilling, energising and freeing if dealt with in the right way. At the same time, it can also become overwhelming, controlling and obsessive if not managed. There is almost a tipping point between good and bad passion, and the line between them is really blurry. Sarah* described this as, *"It's been like the wrong dominoes effect but actually we can make it the right dominoes effect."* It's all about taking control and using the passion energy in the right way. Sometimes this might be as simple as taking some time to reflect on your life and adjust some things, as John* pointed out, *"Might be quite nice to stop for a few days, reorganise everything."*

The good news is that with the right level of self-awareness and ongoing reflection you can learn to keep control of your passion, and use its power in a constructive manner even if it feels overwhelming to start with. There are a further three strategies you can use to help ensure that you avoid the obsessive, negative spiral that can come from an overpowering passion.

Three Strategies to Keep Control of Passion
The first of these is about the kind of goals you set. Goals are great in giving you direction, focus and a destination to head towards. It's easier to make decisions in your life

if you know where you actually want to end up, and goals create these 'ends in sight' to aim towards. Many psychologists and social scientists argue they are also necessary for motivation, engagement and happiness. This makes sense as it's nearly impossible to be driven and successful at something if you don't know why you're doing it or what is the ideal outcome you're looking for. The secret to successfully combining your goal setting with your passion is to set mastery goals in your life and career.

Mastery goals focus on mastering something rather than reaching a specific number or measurement. Their aim is to motivate you to master your life by improving from yesterday to today, and from today to tomorrow. They are all about you becoming the best version of you that you can be, without tying that to specific measures such as income or specific sporting event victories. Contrary to mastery goals, *fixed goals* are tied to fixed things, such as getting a specific promotion, a specific income raise, or a specific amount of sales into your business. These are more likely to lead you into a more obsessive mode and also into a negative spiral if you fail to reach them. Mastery goals include the bigger picture and link success to your improvement rather than to external factors you may be unable to control. And you can always find ways to improve, or understand how you've improved, even by learning through failure.

Mastery goals made a huge difference in my competitive equestrian career once I discovered them. I used to set goals that were tied to specific marks or scores that the judge would give for a specific test I'd ride with my horse. This is how dressage works – it's quite subjective as the marks are defined by what people see and the marks given by the judge are final. The higher the mark, the higher the percentage, the better. However, as with any subjective sport (think gymnastics, figure skating or dance), judges naturally have some kind of subconscious bias regardless of how much they try to avoid it. This means that naturally some judges lean towards specific types of riders or horses because of how they perceive them to be, or perhaps because of their past experiences with them.

This can make dressage quite a frustrating sport as you never quite know how the judge will react to you, your riding and your horse's style. This means that how your ride felt isn't always accurately reflected by the judge's score. When I discovered mastery goals, I completely shifted my perception of how I defined success in the dressage ring. Rather than tying goals to a specific test score, I started tying my goals to mastering a specific movement in the test or a feeling I looked for from my horse. This may sound very abstract, but in fact I knew exactly what I was looking for. And that's the key to setting a mastery goal – as long as you know what 'mastery' feels like to you and you're very specific about it, that's all that matters.

The irony is that with these mastery goals I was able to celebrate every little success more, found more enjoyment from my competitions and actually ended up improving our scores as well! They brought my passion back into the sport as I remembered to enjoy my journey towards mastery. They helped me to stop running all the time, and encouraged me to make time to stop and reflect every now and them. Mastery goals help you do just that – enjoy your journey towards your goals, celebrate every little success on the way, and reflect on your progress continuously. This also helps you keep an eye out for whether the goals continue to be the right ones for you in the space of time, or whether you need to adapt them slightly. When you avoid the obsessive goal trap through mastery goals, you'll remain focused but also flexible and adaptable. This in turn is tied to the sense of freedom that is an outcome of pursuing the passionate way of being, and further fuels it once you discover it.

The second strategy to keep control of your passion is to find a feeling of acceptance and being valued through yourself. Find your authentic self, embrace it, accept it and value it. That is the only way you can truly pursue the passionate way of being and keep control of it. Don't tie your passion to expectations from others or to feeling accepted by others. This can mean you risk diverting your authenticity and sense of passion, or even faking them, just to feel more valued by others. This quickly becomes dangerous as who you're trying to be to please others makes you lose sense of who you truly are. This is when you become a 'pretend you' and start obsessing over the passion that you display and express to others.

Do embrace people's feedback and what they say about you when they see you being your passionate self. But don't tie your passion to that expectation of feedback, or the sense of acceptance that comes with it. This needs to come from deep down within yourself. This is also relevant because in order to progress and master your potential, you need to also be willing to accept constructive feedback. When you find acceptance through your own intrinsic satisfaction, you are more open to and aware of the constructive feedback which will fuel you forward. When you acknowledge the constructive feedback and use it to learn and progress, you are on the path to becoming an expert of your life.[30] Focus on bringing out your passionate self so you can be the best, most authentic version of you that you can be.

The third strategy, which I already touched on a little bit with the mastery goals, is about remaining flexible and adaptable. Sometimes the approach you're using to live and breathe your purpose needs adjustment, or perhaps your goal needs some modifying because some of your circumstances have changed. Sometimes priorities change too, and being aware of this helps you stay connected with your true self and to stay passionate. Life is infinitely dynamic and forever evolving so unexpected things are bound to come up. Learn to thrive in the uncertainty that life brings, and use unexpected twists and turns as learning experiences to grow. Understand that sometimes things don't go as planned and you may need to try something different, or even take a different direction for a bit. As long as you remain self-aware and stay in touch with your authentic self, you'll be able to adapt your path, stay true to your purpose, and live your most passionate life.

When I interviewed George*, he told me there was a point in his life when he felt he had lost control and his sense of freedom because he didn't feel that the life-style he'd built gave him the flexibility he craved. This is a perfect example of how he himself realised that he had tied all his passion to one limiting activity, and this led to him not being able to live his whole life with passion. Through self-awareness and reflection he realised he needed to change his situation to regain control and flexibility. Step by step, this is exactly what he did. Today, the pursuits in his life are aligned with his values and are also more varied. Today, he has the freedom and flexibility to live his whole life with passion.

Say Yes to Passion
I encourage you to say yes to unlocking your passion, to pursuing a passionate way of being, to living your whole life with passion. Say yes to letting your passion help you find your happiest, best performing you who's always filled with energy and a sense of freedom and choice. Say yes to being aware of the magnificence of the positive passion energy, and to continuously checking in with yourself to make sure you're in control of your passion rather than being led by it. Say yes to setting mastery goals so you can fulfil your potential, to finding acceptance and a sense of being valued yourself, and to remaining flexible and adaptable in your pursuits. And

finally, say yes to truly unlocking your positive passion energy by embracing the five passion keys you're about to learn.

Without passion you don't have energy, without energy you have nothing.
~ Donald Trump ~

PART II:

FIVE PASSION KEYS

three

Be the Authentic You

To be yourself in a world that is constantly trying to make you something else is the greatest accomplishment.
~ *Ralph Waldo Emerson* ~

Being the authentic you is the core ingredient in pursuing the passionate way of being. It lays the foundation for you to be able to unlock your inner passion, and express it across different aspects of your life. When you understand who you are, what you stand for, and what drives you, you will naturally bring your passionate self out. This brings us back to the argument of how passion is so much more than a strong feeling towards a particular activity, it's something that is a part of your whole being. Mark* explained this beautifully, saying "*I think it [passion] is more about the identity than just something I do, yeah absolutely.*" You have the opportunity to make the same choice Mark made to make passion a key part of your identity.

Acknowledging that passion is a positive force of energy within you is the first step to awakening it and connecting with it. This comes through a strong sense of self-awareness and needs to happen if you want to learn to choose passion as a way of being so that you can express it across your life. This self-awareness is all about understanding who you are. In order to unlock the passion within you and make it a key component of your identity, you need to understand what your existing identity is made up of. This is why the foundation of the passionate way of being is becoming aware of your authentic self and confidently embracing it every hour of the day, every day of the year.

There are several elements to being the authentic you. The foundation of your authenticity lies in your values and beliefs, which shape the decisions you make in your life. It's important to connect with your values and beliefs because they are one of the most consistent things in your identity throughout your life.[31] Only dramatic life-changing experiences have the power to shift your values, and even then it's often a new value that gets added into your list rather than an elimination of an existing one. Another key component of authenticity is having the courage to be vulnerable. It's only through embracing your emotions, your authentic self and the belief that you're enough just the way you are that makes it possible for you to really bring out your passion with full force.

Being the authentic you not only brings out your passion but also makes it possible for you to build more meaningful connections and perform better, which are both also linked to passion. In a way they all encourage and reinforce each other in a positive spiral. This is why being the real you is the key component in bringing out your most passionate self. Just as you can't sustainably fake who you are without reaching exhaustion and burnout, you also cannot fake the positive passion energy within you. The more wholeheartedly you are able to be yourself and live life according to your true self, the easier it will be to bring out your passion in a natural way. As you start to feel the power of passion cook inside of you, have the courage to keep it cooking and let it influence your decisions in a way that helps you align your whole life around who you are. As Oscar Wilde said, *"Be yourself; everyone else is already taken."*

The Case for Authenticity

Imagine you had to be someone else for a day. Imagine you had to adopt their look, their style and how they spoke. You would be forced to take on their values and beliefs, and base every small and big decision on them. You would have to eat, drink, sleep, walk and move exactly how they did. You would have to do every little thing exactly how they would do them – from the way you picked up the pen to write to the way you interacted with your colleagues to the way you kissed your partner. How do you think you would feel after 24 hours of being somebody else?

The initial novel excitement of pretending to be someone else and living their life would wear off quickly, and you'd realise how challenging it is to pretend to be someone else. It would take a huge toll on your energy levels, and you'd feel both mentally and physically drained. Every thought or action would be accompanied with a strong sense of resistance, and you'd have to force every cell in your body and brain to behave in a way that they're not used to, or even built to, behave. You would be going against your natural way of being. The more this *pretend person* would be different from you, the more deflated you would feel at the end of this day as you would be clashing aggressively with the authentic you. This is a sure way to prevent your passion from coming out.

Situations like these rip away the passion from your life. Yes, there may be moments in your life that you may need to adapt your behaviour based on the audience, the situation and the circumstances – but never at the expense of being someone who you're not. This is one of the reasons why unhappiness and disengagement in the workplace continues to be a problem in today's age.[32] When you decide to leave the real you outside the office you are setting yourself up for an uphill struggle.

You cannot sustain your motivation, energy or drive at work if you're not being the real you because you're spending every ounce of energy you have to fight the real you from coming out. You're basically going into the office every day acting – which professional actors and actresses can confirm is not healthy or sustainable for 24 hours a day 365 days a year. You're basically setting yourself up not only for disengagement at work but also for burnout, – especially if you're still trying to perform at your best at work. It's time to change the belief that you have to leave your authentic self outside the office door. It's time you took it in with you – and everywhere else in your life.

When you say to yourself, "*I'll be the real me with my family*", or "*when I'm doing my favourite hobby*", or "*once I become a Senior Manager*", you're asking for trouble. You cannot truly separate who you are in different aspects of your life because you are one whole being and you take your whole being with you everywhere you go. You can try to fight certain elements of it, or suppress them, but this will only lead to frustration and tension in your subconscious and in your physical being. When you're saying that you'll be *the real you* once you get to a specific position in your career or life, you're delaying your happiness. You'll also risk losing sense of who you truly are because you'll be living a lie for so long you'll struggle to separate the real you from the pretend you. When you do all these things to fight with your authentic self, you're saying no to passion and no to fulfilment. In essence, you're saying no to living your life fully. And who wants to do that?

We only get to live life once, and many argue it's too short already to do all the things we want to do. So why waste any second of it pretending to be someone you're not? Truly forget about who you should be, and be who you truly are. It's your unique self that helps drive progress and innovation in the world, because only you can make a difference in the world in your own way. It's the unique you that brings out your natural talents, which not only help you perform at your best and find fulfilment, but they also help create positive change and inspire others to be their authentic selves. It's this authentic self, and connection with it, that makes it possible for you to unlock your inner passion.

In Alignment with Your Values
In order to live life authentically and connect with your inner passion, it is essential for you to understand the values that are most important to you. Values are the ideologies, principles or standards of behaviour that you find important.[33] It's your personal judgement of what is important in life, and hence you can define your values however you want to, making them completely unique to you. They are the principles that help you prioritise what you need and what you base most of your decisions on. They often become most clear when you are faced with big decisions that are going to affect your lifestyle and long-term plans. You often weigh your options against your values.

For example, my top values are achievement, expertise, passion, gratitude and quality. This means that I'm driven by making things happen and by becoming the best I can possibly be in the field that I am in. I am very committed to living a life that brings my positive passion energy out and is aligned with who I am and what I enjoy doing. I relish taking time to appreciate everything in my life and show my gratitude to others. Last but not least, quality is always a big priority for me as I have a borderline anal attention to detail which is accompanied by high standards – both when it comes to things I deliver and also to what I expect from others. These are the five values I take with me wherever I go and whenever I have an important decision to make.

Despite deciding to not pursue riding dressage professionally, I'm still very committed to the sport. I have ambitious goals I set in the competitive arena, and I want to become an expert in riding my horse in the best possible way. I train with some of the best trainers in the country whose passion and commitment to the sport instantaneously rub off on me. When I work with clients through my Happyologist training business, I make sure that the clients I work with appreciate the expertise, passion and quality I bring to the table. I choose to work on projects that have the power to create real positive change so that I can find a sense of achievement through them.

Recognising your values helps you take them with you wherever you go, and to build a life that's coherent with them. Sometimes the first step of awareness can already light the positive passion energy within you as you realise how you've subconsciously made decisions based on your values and hence built a life aligned with your true self. Other times simply asking yourself how you can take these values with you everywhere you go can already help you realise how you can make minuscule changes that will have a big effect. Sometimes all that's needed is a shift in perception or perspective. The exercises at the end of this chapter will help you work through this.

The discussion around authenticity and values ties us back to Aristotle's philosophical origins of passion as well as the current psychological research around eudaimonic happiness. Aristotle spoke of the passion that arose when you were in alignment with your true self, and 21st-century positive psychologists have expanded this alignment with your true self as being the core ingredient of eudaimonic happiness.[34] This type of happiness is also connected to a sense of self-realisation and personal growth, both of which are linked to authenticity, values and the passionate way of being. As you become more aware of your values, you are able to express them in a way that leads to greater wellbeing and more fulfilling personal growth.[35] Both of these are key drivers of the passionate way of being.

Even before the age of positive psychology, Alan Waterman spoke of personal expressiveness, defining it as a life full of activities that are connected with your deeply held values.[36] He highlighted how it is the holistic engagement in different activities and being aware of their connection to your values that drives this sense of authenticity. He spoke about how living life according to your values makes you feel intensely alive, and that you exist exactly how you are meant to exist. He's referring to the same positive sense of energy that comes out when you fully live and breathe the passionate way of being.

Living congruently with your values not only brings out your passion but also positively affects your wellbeing. Research has also suggested that the more intrinsic, achievement-orientated values (such as excitement, self-expression and passion) are more conducive to your wellbeing than those driven by extrinsic factors (such as tradition or stability).[37] Living a life in alignment with your authentic values also brings a sense of autonomy and internal drive to reach your goals, and even makes you more creative in solving challenges on the journey to achieving your goals.[38] As you can see, the authentic values that connect you with your passion also connect you with wellbeing and motivation. It's a win-win in so many ways!

It's important to have an idea of your most important values that shape the key decisions in your life. The more you are able to become aware of them, the more you are able to align your decisions with them and create a life that fuels your positive passion energy. Recognising how you prioritise them will also help you use them in different situations and contexts as it's natural for their importance to sometimes shift in a different life domain. You will have an opportunity to play with this a little bit later in this chapter.

Understanding Your Beliefs
Your beliefs can be tied to your values but can be more extrinsically driven. Whereas values are something that are quite internal to you and consistent throughout your life, your beliefs can be influenced by the environment you're in and can shift in different phases in your life. Your beliefs are influenced by the cultures you've been exposed to, the type of society you live in, the ideas that your family has passed on to you, and the experiences

you have had in your life. Beliefs are not as deeply held as your values, which are a core part of your being, but instead they are more like assumptions and perceptions that you have and that you believe to be true.

Being aware of your beliefs makes it possible for you to behave in an authentic way that connects with your passion through your current assumption. Just as much as life is dynamic and forever evolving, so are you and your beliefs. This means awareness around them is even more critical so that you are not living life according to your past beliefs or beliefs that someone else has imposed on you. Living according to your present, true beliefs is what makes that positive passion energy come out of you and fires you up for the activities that you choose to do.

For example, I used to believe that a quiet life in the countryside was something I wanted because I genuinely thought it was a part of who I was. I thought waking up in the morning seeing fields and horses was my dream, and that I wanted to build an online business that I could easily run from my own bedroom. Somehow, these were the beliefs that I had got into my head because I'd always loved horses and thought I wanted the flexibility to be with them 24/7. But this belief changed quickly after a life-changing event in my personal life made me realise this was a belief that was driven more by *should* than by real desire. I understood that a life in the countryside also represented peace and quiet for me, yet what I truly needed was to find peace and quiet within myself. A life in the countryside was just a facade representation of external peace and quiet when in fact I needed to find it within. This realisation made me completely change my belief in what kind of life I craved, and the decisions that followed helped me shape my new lifestyle according to who I truly was and what I truly wanted.

This highlights how a core element of understanding your beliefs is also understanding who you believe yourself to be. This brings us back to Waterman's idea of personal expressiveness, in which he highlighted that people who live their lives according to their values and beliefs also believe this is who they are and what they are meant to do.[39] Other psychologists have also tied feeling a sense of authenticity to embracing the belief that this is who you are.[40]

Being authentic to your values and beliefs isn't simply about being aware of them, but actually making choices and living life according to them. It's about believing in who you are and what you're meant to do. It's only with this belief and confidence in yourself that you are able to fully open up the passion energy that's within you. That's where vulnerability has a big role to play.

Vulnerability and Courage
Authenticity isn't always easy. It takes real courage. You need to have courage to be the real you, to express your real emotions, to share the real you with the world. You might be scared of showing your real self because you're afraid of getting hurt, of not being accepted, of not finding a sense of belonging. You might feel exposed and naked when you're sharing the real you with the world.

But it's time you overcame that fear, because it's only when you're being the real vulnerable you that you're truly alive. It's only then that you can connect with the positive passion energy within you.

Brené Brown has done inspirational work on vulnerability that has really put a new type of courage on the map. It's no surprise that her TED talk[41] is one of most viewed talks on the TED.com site, which hosts inspirational talks about ideas worth spreading – make sure to check it out if you haven't yet (and also check out her book *Daring Greatly*)![42] She talks about how vulnerability not only connects you with your courage and your authentic self, but also helps you build meaningful connections with people. In her research she talks about wholehearted people who live from a deep sense of worthiness. These people have the courage to be the real them, despite their imperfections. They have the courage to have self-compassion, and be kind to themselves so they can be kinder to others. They let go of who they should be and truly embrace who they really are. They believe that being vulnerable is what makes them beautiful.

This is the vulnerability you need to wholeheartedly take up in order to fully connect with your authentic self and your inner passion. You need to be brave and let yourself to be deeply seen. You need to have the courage to love with your whole heart, and use your emotions throughout your life, despite not having any guarantees of what you'll get back. You need to practise gratitude and joy in moments of terror and uncertainty. Most of all, you need to believe you're enough, you need to be kinder and gentler to you so that you can be kinder and gentler to those around you.

It's this sense of vulnerability which helps you find your real self, to connect with it and to accept it. This connection and belief in it will help unlock that passion that lies within you as you realise how to connect with your core being. That's when you start to make decisions based on your values and beliefs, and you will not only feel the passion come alive but you'll also discover a new-found sense of courage. You will learn to accept your strengths and weaknesses, and discover how to be compassionate towards yourself. You will believe in yourself in a whole new way, finding a voice you never had. You'll see challenges as opportunities to learn, and you'll be ready to jump in at the deep end, knowing that you'll be able to swim and survive. So be brave, be vulnerable, be you. Because that's what will bring you your passion and help you live your most fulfilling life. And that's what you're worthy of.

Bringing the Real You to Work

A unique discussion in today's society is whether to bring the real you to work. There seems to be a misconception that you can't bring the real you to work because you can't display your real emotions at work. Both of these ideas work against your passion, happiness and performance – both inside and outside the workplace. Let's start with the idea of bringing an alter ego to work.

As I already mentioned earlier, pretending to be someone you're not in the office is a dangerous strategy. You will find it harder to stay motivated, energised and successful if you're continuously wasting your energy on acting like someone else. You will struggle to find enjoyment in your role and you will end every day exhausted. You won't be able to create real connections or relationships with the people in your workplace, again limiting your enjoyment at work. These will all further contribute to a lack of energy, motivation and performance as you struggle to act like someone else. Your passion will be hiding deep inside of you with no sign of it coming out to see daylight.

I remember going through this myself in my corporate career. As an employee driven by achievement, passion and quality, I was still putting 100% into my role even though I had realised it wasn't what I actually wanted. I was still committed to meeting my goals, to delivering exceptional work, and to enjoying it as much as I could. At this point I had already started to build my Happyologist business idea on the side so I knew there was an end in sight. But I ended most of my work days so exhausted I could barely find any energy to work on my Happyologist idea. I was working on things I didn't really believe in, I didn't feel appreciated in my role and I felt there was a values clash between myself and the organisation I worked for. I was running myself to the ground trying my best to still deliver exceptional work even though I didn't necessarily believe in it.

I then had a real eureka moment as I woke up one Wednesday morning and all of a sudden the whole room was spinning. I didn't know where the walls, ceiling or floor were – they were all a big blur. I felt like I was in a washing machine. Somehow I managed to scramble into the bathroom with the help of my then boyfriend to throw up numerous times and then go back to lying on the floor. Any slight movement made everything spin. When the paramedics arrived they gave me some magical pills to help me stop spinning but the real cure was bed rest. It took me a whole two weeks to recover fully. I had got acute vertigo from the stress at work. At the age of 24. Only two years into my corporate career. This was not a good sign. But it was a sign that I was on the wrong path, exhausting myself pretending to be someone else at work.

Today, my Happyologist business is aligned with every value and belief I have, and I work with clients who follow very similar ideologies. I use my natural strengths in the work that I do, and make sure that I'm having fun most of the time. I work hard and sometimes long hours during busy times but because the work I do is so aligned with who I am, it doesn't drain me or exhaust me the way my corporate career used to do.

Now that's not to say entrepreneurship or a new career is the key to lighting your passion – not at all! I believe you can truly find love in what you do as long as you understand how it's aligned with your true self. My first role in my corporate career was an amazing experience. Even though the role itself was not my first choice, the sense of appreciation I got from my team was through the roof, the friendships I made with my ambitious colleagues were truly inspiring, and the values my manager used to lead and motivate us were almost 100% aligned with mine. So I was able to find a happy medium in the role because I was able to understand how what I was doing and the environment I was in was still aligned with who I was and what I believed in.

I was also able to express my emotions quite openly (in a diplomatic way) and the leaders in the organisation I worked in encouraged this. This is where emotional intelligence comes in. It doesn't mean wearing your emotions on your sleeve, but being aware of your real emotions and using them wisely while still being authentic. Daniel Goleman is one of the founding fathers and leading researchers in the field of emotional intelligence, and he has found how becoming self-aware of your emotions makes you more able to do good work.[43] Because you realise how you feel when you are doing different things, you'll be able to better navigate your life in and out of the workplace and find natural focus towards things you're good at.

Being connected with your emotions in the workplace also helps you manage them better. For example, if you find yourself becoming frustrated by a particular challenge, ask yourself why you're becoming frustrated. Do you believe it should be approached from a different angle? You don't think you're the best person to solve the challenge? Or maybe you just can't find any enjoyment in the challenge. Once you have an idea of what it is, then you are much more able to resolve it, or to ask someone for help with how to resolve it. It's when we suppress our emotions, or leave them outside the workplace, that problems arise as you can't simply pretend to shut emotions off. They're much more likely to then affect us through our subconscious in a negative way.

The more helpful way to deal with your emotions is to take them with your authentic self into the office, and be aware of them so that you can more effectively manage them. This awareness around your emotions will help you to focus on the positive emotions and use them as fuel for yourself. It's through connecting with your emotional energy, and focusing on the right type of energy, that will make it possible for you to tap into the positive passion energy that's lying inside of you ready to come out.

Putting Authenticity into Action

Staying in touch with your authentic self is an ongoing dynamic process. The more self-aware you are, the more able you will be to make decisions and live your life according to the real you. There is only one catch. Just like life and everything around you, you are in a constant state of change. That means that some of your beliefs, assumptions or ideologies might change over your life (even though your values are most likely to stay consistent). Hence you need to make an effort to continuously check back on your changing self and forever evolving being.

Daniel Gilbert talks about this 'constant state of change' phenomenon in his book *Stumbling on Happiness*, thoroughly arguing the case for how human beings are never-ending works in progress.[44] This is another argument for not finding or following 'a one passion' because it is quite likely to change over time.

This is what makes living your whole life with passion so beautiful and so opportunistic. You can forever continue progressing and evolving throughout your life, and you can take this passionate way of being wherever you go no matter what you do. The only thing for you to remember is to keep checking back on who is the authentic you right now, and how you can make the decisions that help you live a life that's most aligned with your current self. Equally, through working on your self-awareness and your authenticity, you will be able to create new perceptions of the world that show how some components of your life are already aligned with who you are. This sense of awareness is the first step to igniting the passion spark inside of you.

Discovering Your Authentic Passionate Way of Being
As you learn to live your life through pursuing this passionate way of being, it's likely that you will find that this positive passion energy has been in there all along. As I interviewed Albert* through my research, he discovered exactly that:

> *You realise it's something that has echoed all the way back through your life so you kind of then can draw a line through and say 'Ahaa, yes this is, this is who I've been all along'.*

Now it's time for you to start discovering your passionate way of being through tapping into your authentic self. I'm going to take you through three questions that will help you to explore your real self, identify whether your life is in alignment with who you are, and show you how to better incorporate your real self into your life right now.

1. What are my top five values that I base important decisions on?

A value is any ideology or principle you really want to live your life by. Some examples of values include:

- ✓ Achievement
- ✓ Acknowledgement
- ✓ Appreciation of beauty
- ✓ Compassion
- ✓ Equality
- ✓ Excellence
- ✓ Expertise
- ✓ Freedom
- ✓ Forgiveness
- ✓ Honesty
- ✓ Humour
- ✓ Humility
- ✓ Independence
- ✓ Integrity
- ✓ Learning
- ✓ Passion
- ✓ Persistence
- ✓ Perspective
- ✓ Quality
- ✓ Recognition
- ✓ Respect
- ✓ Truth

> **EXERCISE:**
> Think about a time when you were at your happiest, most proud, or most fulfilled and satisfied. Why did these positive emotions (e.g. joy, pride, love) come out in that particular situation?

Understanding a very positive experience from your past helps you shine light on what it is that is important to you because it's very likely that positive experience matched or highlighted some of your top values to you.

For example, one of my happiest and proudest moments was when I took my young horse Mickey to his first four-year-old competition. It was his first ever competition, my first ever young horse class, and it was also my first Premier League competition (a prestigious dressage series in Great Britain). I had owned Mickey for a year by then, and had trained him myself (with the help of my trainers) from when he was just under three years old, barely ridden in. I was very nervous (and possibly quite terrified!) of riding this powerful, spirited young horse at this competition as I didn't quite know what to expect. After the initial five minutes of showing off in the warm-up ring, he calmed down and listened to me very closely. As I went in to ride the test in front of the judges (behind a professional Grand Prix rider!), I was more confident and focused myself. He behaved impeccably in front of the judges and we got a very promising score to finish eighth out of 36 riders in a very tough class – I was ecstatic.

But what I remember the most is the wave of emotions that came over me as I finished the test, gave him long reins and gave him a big pat on the neck. I had never been so proud or happy in my life. I was one with my horse, and one with the values that mattered to me. I was one with achievement, as I had achieved a huge step in my riding and reached a massive stretch of a goal. I was one with passion, as I felt the positive energy run through me as I was doing something I truly loved, feeling the special bond I had with my horse. I was one with expertise, as I felt how I had improved in my riding to get to this stage and excelled in the class dominated by professionals.

EXERCISE:
Now think of a time when you were particularly frustrated or annoyed in a situation where someone else didn't behave as you expected. Why were you frustrated?

Exploring a time when you were frustrated or annoyed can also highlight some of your most important values to you. Often when you get especially annoyed when other people don't behave as you expect, they're behaving in a way that's in conflict with your values. You feel disrespected because you feel as if your values and beliefs are not being acknowledged. This is completely natural but it's important to also acknowledge that everyone has different values and beliefs, and there is no right or wrong in that. The more self-aware you become, the more you're able to manage your emotions in situations like this and also understand other people's values.

For example, I was pitching my Happyologist training offerings to a big financial company a few years ago. I met up with two very senior leaders in the organisation and explained the science behind what I do. I shared some of the workshop outlines with them and they seemed to like the sound of them. Everything seemed to be moving in the right direction until one of them explicitly said, *"We don't want you to be too inspirational. We can't let the people think too much because then they might leave."* Imagine the shock when I heard that! I tried my best to keep a poker face and remain diplomatic, though in reality I had nearly fallen off my chair in shock. I went on to explain how if people end up leaving, that's a good thing because you're getting rid of people who are already disengaged and you can get someone who's much more motivated and driven into the role. Despite this, I felt I wouldn't be able to deliver my workshops on a free enough rein so I decided to turn the company away because of a value mismatch. I felt they didn't trust or appreciate the expertise I was bringing to the table, and I felt I wouldn't be able to deliver the high quality of work I insist on delivering if I was asked to modify my training content or approach too much.

2. How does my life and career reflect my values and beliefs?

The two areas in the question (life and career) should be worked on separately. They will give you a good first impression of whether there is more of your real self in your life outside of work, or whether your authentic self is healthily present at your work as well.

EXERCISE:
Start by looking at your life outside work overall. How do you carry your values and beliefs with you everywhere you go?

Reflecting on whether you find yourself making decisions based on your values across different aspects of your life will help give you a helicopter view of whether you're living a life true to who you are. Yes, it's true that some decisions (like deciding which milk to buy in the supermarket) don't need to engage your values but bigger lifestyle decisions, such as choosing where to live, what job offer to accept, and how to spend your weekend, need to reflect your values if you want to live a life with passion.

For example, when I finished my undergraduate degree at university, I had two offers from two very different organisations to join their two-year graduate scheme. Having just finished my studies and not having had a permanent job before, I was quite confused about how to decide. They were both well-known companies though one offered more international career opportunities than the other. Location wise, one was in quite a rural area and the other had its main offices in big cities or in the outskirts of big cities. They were in completely different industries though both sold consumer products. One was very exclusive and the other more everyday use. They both offered great learning opportunities and a strong training scheme that would help me develop my skills thoroughly. I only had about four days to make the decision as the deadline to accept the offer for one of them was shortly after I received the second offer. I had to find a way to decide quickly and efficiently how I wanted to start my career.

This is where my values came in. I thought about what was important to me and how aligned the company values were with mine. I thought about whether my desire for achievement would be met, if I'd be able to become an expert in what I'd do, and how I'd be appreciated as an employee. I thought about which of the companies would naturally bring more passion out of me through enjoyment, and which of them was more aligned with high quality. Even when I explored this tough decision through my values, I still struggled because two of the values were clear in one company and three in the other. I made the decision to go with the one which aligned with three of my values, and made sure that every role I had in the company I'd be able to bring in my other two somehow. And at the start it definitely worked. The first role I had in the organisation taught me a lot about not only what I was doing, but also about myself and what I actually wanted to do. I was surrounded by colleagues who respected my values and a manager who knew how to motivate me through them.

The second role in the organisation was a bit more shaky and made it clear how lucky I had been in my first role. The third year was when I started to realise things in the organisation had changed and that it no longer fitted with my values. In my three years in this corporation I did my best to carry my values with me in any way I could. However, when I felt my values were no longer being respected enough, I made the decision it was time to move on to set up my Happyologist business. In hindsight, I could have spoken about this challenge more openly with my team to try to resolve it, and I encourage you to do that if you are feeling there is a mismatch. Despite my choice to leave, I left with an incredible sense of gratitude for how the company had helped me grow as an employee and as a person. After all, a lot of what I learned there I have been able to put into use in my own business and when working with corporate clients.

EXERCISE:
Now look at your life at work. How do you carry your values and beliefs with you in every role you have in the workplace?

You have the opportunity to bring your values and beliefs to the work you do. In every role that you have throughout your career, you can discover how it's aligned with some of your values. This is one of the basic ways for you to unlock your passion at work and become more driven and motivated there.

For example, even when I was in the corporate world and not entirely satisfied with my role there, I discovered I could still find a sense of achievement by committing to projects and helping my team reach important milestones. I realised that by sharing my gratitude more with my team and department, I got more of it back. I still committed to delivering high quality work whatever I did, and I aimed for expertise as I looked for new ways to succeed as I worked on new projects.

You have the same choice in your current role. Even if you realise that the company values are not an exact match with your values, or that the role you're working on isn't giving you enjoyment, you can actually find more joy, productivity and passion by creating these ties with your values. If you're in an organisation or team that is built on trust and open communication, you could talk to your manager or colleagues about what your values are and how you'd like them to be incorporated into how you work. Perhaps there is even an opportunity to join a project that would help you live out your values more. Often, with clear communication and an open mind, you'll find new approaches to your existing role that can help you find more joy and satisfaction in it. In essence, that will bring out your passionate self and help you find love in what you do.

3. How could I better incorporate my values into the decisions and actions I take in my life?

The first step in bringing out your inner passion through authenticity is awareness of your values and beliefs. The second step is reflecting on how your life already reflects those values and beliefs. The final step is about exploring how you could incorporate more of your values into how you live your life.

> **EXERCISE:**
> What can you do to remind yourself to check in with your values in more of the decisions you take in your life?

It could be that you are already happy with how your values reflect your life and you might feel confident that they are always in the back (or front) of your mind when you make decisions. It could also be that you are satisfied with how you bring your values to some aspects of your life, but you'd like to bring them more into others. If you struggle with this question, have a look at some coaching questions in the Cheat Sheet (page 233) at the back of the book to help you think out of the box.

For example, I can confidently say the lifestyle I've built strongly reflects my top five values. Both the work I do through my Happyologist business and the training I commit to in the dressage sport I truly love heavily reflect my values and are always influenced by them. On the other hand, when it comes to committing time and energy into taking care of myself or even simply resting, my values are not reflected enough there. As a very goal- and deadline-driven person, I struggle to allow myself to rest at the end of the working day if I don't have an achievement to celebrate.

Yes, I eat healthily, sleep plenty and get lots of exercise. But I'm still learning to bring in my values when it comes to rest and relaxation. I'm still learning to appreciate the time and energy I commit to my business and riding, learning to allocate more 'high quality relaxation time' for myself, and learning to become an expert in mentally switching off at the end of the working day (e.g. think meditation and mindfulness exercises). I now have a 'success file' on my laptop that has positive messages and testimonials from happy clients and encouraging quotes from my riding trainers. I look at that at the end of the working day if I feel like I haven't achieved enough, and in a weird way it gives me permission to finish work for the day and relax. I have downloaded a few guided meditations to my mobile so I can listen to them when I know I need to refocus and unwind. I have made a commitment to have one evening a week just to myself doing whatever I feel like doing to recharge.

If you want to pursue the passionate way of being and live a fulfilling, passionate, high energy life, making time for relaxation and recharging is critical. Even though you're mentally energised through living life with passion, you still get tired physically and you still need time to rest (as any human being would!). As you've seen here, even your values can play a role in how you approach that.

Embrace the Authentic Passionate You
The first step to unlocking your inner passion is starting to live life as your authentic self. Forget about who

you should be, but be who you truly want to be. Cherish your values and beliefs, make decisions based on them, and live life carrying them with you wherever you go. These are the key points to remember from being authentic:

1. Identify what your values are and you will have a better understanding of what is important to you and why. Being aware of your values and fully embracing them is the first step to unlocking your passion.

2. Have the courage to carry your values with you wherever you go and share them openly with the world when you see fit. This will help you to appreciate how some of the activities and things in your life already reflect your values. This in turn will light up that positive passion energy in activities you didn't even realise you enjoyed and/or found value in.

3. Acknowledge that being the authentic you at work is what helps you to be your best performing, most passionate you. Think about how you can be more of the real you at work by exploring how you could bring your values into the work you do in a more comprehensive way.

When you learn to embrace the authentic you, and truly believe in yourself, that passion within you will naturally start to surface. Especially when you start to realise how what you do is already somewhat (or fully) aligned with who you are. In one of the scenes in the film *The Legend of Bagger Vance*, inspirational golf caddy Bagger says something to the golfer about his swing that cleverly highlights the idea how there is that unique, authentic self in each and everyone one of us. He said:

Inside each and every one of us is one true authentic swing...
Somethin' we was born with...
Somethin' that's ours and ours alone...
Somethin' that can't be taught to ya or learned...
Somethin' that got to be remembered...
Over time the world can, rob us of that swing...
It get buried inside us under all our
wouldas and couldas and shouldas ...[45]

I encourage you to let go of your *wouldas, couldas and shouldas,* and embrace the real, authentic you that makes you unique. Embrace it, and you will feel your passion light up inside of you.

four

Find Your Why

*Passion is energy. Feel the power that comes
from focusing on what excites you.*
~ Oprah Winfrey ~

The second key component to pursuing the passionate way
of being in your life is understanding the bigger picture.
It's about exploring and getting an idea of what your core
purpose in life is. It's about exploring the kind of positive
impact you want to create, be it through your personal con-
tacts or in the wider scheme of things. It's about realising
how you want to contribute to the world. Understanding
your purpose means consciously knowing what is the why
behind what you do and carrying it with you wherever you
go. It's the thing that inspires you to work towards things
and gives you a direction in life. It's the thing that motivates
you to jump out of bed in the morning excited. This is the
same thing that ignites the passion energy within you.

You might think that there is time for you to think
about your purpose tomorrow, or next year, or when

you're in a more comfortable situation financially, or even when you're retired and you can commit your full attention to a good cause. But those are the wrong approaches to take in life. Just as delaying your authentic self causes stress, unhappiness and exhaustion, so does delaying finding your why. And delays are not good because time is a limited resource in this world. Time is the only thing that is equal to everyone. We all have 60 seconds in a minute, 60 minutes in an hour, 24 hours in a day. No matter who you are, how much you make or what you do, you still only have 24 hours a day.

Time is a finite resource and its power over you is easily forgotten. You cannot buy time, you cannot borrow it, you cannot create it. You cannot pause it, slow it down or speed it up. The time you have is the time you have. That's outside your control. But what you can control is how you spend your time. And the more clearly you understand your why, the easier it is to spend your time in a wise way that not only creates positive impact but also brings out your passionate self. This passionate self in turn will help you find more fulfilment, happiness, sense of freedom and energy (as already discussed in Chapter Two).

The reason I encourage you to think about your why today and not tomorrow is because you don't know what comes tomorrow. A well-known Swedish engineer and innovator – let's call him Sven for now – makes a point about this through his story. When Sven was 55 years old, one of his brothers passed away and the newspapers mistakenly published Sven's obituary instead of his brother's thinking that Sven had passed away. One of the obituaries in a French newspaper was titled, "The merchant of death is dead", and went on further to say, "Dr. Sven, who became rich by finding a way to kill the most amount of people faster than ever before, died yesterday". The newspaper was referring to Sven's invention of dynamite. So can you guess who Sven is? Dr. Alfred Nobel.

When Dr. Alfred Nobel read this obituary which was published by mistake, he was horrified. Was this how he was going to be remembered? Was this the legacy he was leaving behind? That's when he decided to donate 94% of his fortune to set up the Nobel Prize foundation. Today, that's how we remember his name and that's how he is known – for encouraging and rewarding development and progress in the fields of science, literature and society.

Nobel got a second chance to re-brand himself and think of his why, but he got lucky. His re-evaluation of his own life in the last stage of his life made it possible for him to change his purpose and his legacy last minute. But it's unlikely you will get that chance. And even if you would, why would you want to wait to the last stage of your life to pursue it? Don't waste any second of your life working towards things you don't feel connected to. This is a sure way to block your passion and fulfilment in life, as well as your performance. It's time you embraced the real you and reflected on the why behind what you do.

What is a 'Why'
Your why is the purpose you believe you want to fulfil in your life. It's the reason behind everything you do, and

it's the thing that drives you into action. It's something that's completely unique to you and something you live your life by, regardless of what other people have to say. The people I interviewed about passion spoke about how their why and their desire to have a positive impact ignited their passion. Here are some of the ways they described their why:

> - *"I am driven by seeing this kind of beautiful thing work, but I'm also driven by this maximum impact"*.
> - *"I would like to think that whatever I do will make a positive difference to whichever area I'm working in"*.
> - *"[I want to be] making a difference basically. Making an impact, or something like that"*.

As you can see the common denominator with all their why's was about making some kind of difference through what they do. Another interviewee spoke about how they use the 'why' approach for all their ideas: *"Ideas have to have good quality to them so the thing we're doing is purposeful."* They incorporated 'why' as a mechanism to assess their ideas to ensure that everything that they were doing had a purpose behind it.

Having a purpose behind what you do doesn't mean that you need to aim to be the leader of your country to resolve all its challenges. It doesn't mean that you have to work in a charity that focuses on a cause that is supported by everyone (think Save the Children). It doesn't mean you need to work towards saving the planet so we can secure a more sustainable future for the future generations. It simply means that you understand what is your motivation for doing things and what is the kind of positive impact you want to create. Understanding how you are creating positive impact is what motivates human beings because it gives you a clear sense of purpose. It makes what you do worthwhile. It makes you feel a part of something bigger. This is also what makes the world progress forward. Everyone has the potential to make their unique mark on the world through the kind of positive impact they create. Including you.

Your why is often tied to your values because the only way you can connect with it is by ensuring it's in alignment with your authentic self. It's important that the way you choose to fulfil this why enables you to stay true to your values, otherwise you will create more conflict and distress in your life. For example, my why is to educate and inspire people to choose happiness, passion and success in their lives. How I choose to fulfil this why could go in a million different directions, but I want to make sure that through whatever I do I find a sense of achievement, expertise and gratitude. To me the ideal answer was to build a business that would enable exactly that. With every talk, workshop or coaching session I do through Happyologist, I get a sense of achievement as I see the eyes of my clients light up as they understand what I'm talking about. With every positive feedback and thank you note I get, I feel I am appreciated and equally feel a sense of gratitude to be able to do work that helps other people in their lives. With every client project and constructive feedback I receive, I'm always looking to improve what I offer and keep it very high quality. In line with this, I also keep up to date on the latest research in the field to aim for expertise in everything I do.

This overarching why I have, to show people how they can choose happiness and passion, runs throughout my life. From my business to my riding to my social life. Everywhere I go, I am naturally spreading this message and stepping in to help whenever and wherever I can. This is my focus and this is what gives me direction in my everyday life. This is also how the people in my research described it. For example, one participant said: *"What I'm trying to say is that my heart is very in tune with my passion, and that I'm making sure that is in tune with my actual practical everyday life"*. Even though this why may dominate one area of your life, it can also take different shapes in different areas of your life.

For example, my why comes across very clearly through my business, but I also spread the message through my blog, which anyone can read to get inspired. I also choose to share my knowledge, or give helpful tips, to the people I know in the horse world (it's surprising how powerful some of this stuff is, even when it comes to dealing with horses!). In my social life, I've made the commitment to be the positive, passionate soul in the room who aims to lift everyone's energy and helps them work towards their dreams.

Equally, you can have slightly different adaptations of your why when it comes to different areas of your life. Research is showing that it is incredibly common to be multifaceted with your values and how you find meaning in different areas of your life, because what you value and find meaningful in one area of your life is different from what you value and find meaningful in another.[46] However, having an overarching sense of purpose that's somewhat coherent with all of them helps you integrate these adaptations of your why into your life in an authentic way. For example, it could be that your purpose is to drive creativity forward through collaboration. In the workplace this could mean you do specific things that encourage collaboration and cooperation through your team (or the organisation). Outside work you could reflect the same purpose by running brainstorming sessions with friends or your network to innovate around challenges at work and in life. It could be that with your partner you master how to collaborate when it comes to splitting housework and having fun while doing it. These might sound like simple, insignificant things but it's surprising how uplifting and energising it is to live your life with a clear why.

It's especially important to remember here that you can bring in an adaptation of your why to any job you do. In fact, this is key to finding happiness at work as you learn to connect with it meaningfully. It is also the key to motivation and performance because your authentic why will light up your passion also in the workplace. Some of my clients have spoken about their values of love and kindness, and often argued they weren't relevant in the workplace. I believe practically every why can be transferred into your workplace (without going into extremes), even if your why is to spread more love and kindness in the world. Maybe you want to inspire and help your colleagues to build better relationships with each other through kindness and compassion (which is a form of love). Not only would this bring out your passion in the workplace, it would also have huge benefits for the business. One of the key drivers of happiness and performance at work is positive relationships,[47] and with this why you could be the enabler of that if you wanted.

Perhaps if you're in a leadership role, and your why is in helping people reach their potential, your purpose at work could be to encourage people to develop and grow as much as possible. If you are very committed to inspiring others to be their true selves, and to embrace and appreciate diversity everywhere you go, at work you could aim to create an environment of trust where people feel comfortable to be themselves and speak their mind.

You can have a 'key why' that drives everything you do in life, or sometimes you may have a few different whys in different areas of your life. This is especially common for parents (and grandparents) who often feel their why is to provide their children with the best possible opportunities in life. In fact, research has repeatedly shown that being a parent provides a lot of meaning in your life.[48] If this is the case with you, it's important to still remember your overarching why, reflect on whether it's changed, and stay in alignment with your authentic self with whichever why you decide to commit to.

Having an overarching purpose that crosses over to all domains of your life is very rewarding, and can sometimes be easier to manage. Start reflecting on what your key why could be, and the other 'sub-whys' that could walk alongside it. Later on in this chapter you'll be able to explore this in depth through numerous exercises.

Purpose and Passion
Having a sense of purpose through understanding your why doesn't simply unlock your passion and help you connect with a bigger cause. It also provides you with a more meaningful type of happiness. This is what psychologists refer to as eudaimonic happiness (as I already introduced earlier in the book).

Hence it's no surprise that recent reports have found that the so-called *millennial generation* looks for meaning more than money when it comes to creating a successful career.[49] They have the desire to make a difference through what they do. They want to feel that their lives and careers have purpose, value and impact. They want to feel connected to something bigger than the self. They have understood that leading a meaningful life would help them feel connected to others, to their careers, to a life purpose, and to the world itself. They seem to have truly understood the value of creating a life that incorporates the seeds of eudaimonic happiness – and passion!

Research has shown that one of the key drivers of satisfaction and engagement at work is feeling a sense of purpose.[50] Yet so many people are going into their jobs and living their lives without understanding their whys. They are getting through the everyday without having a clear sense of the direction they are heading in. Understanding your why gives you an idea of your direction, or at least sets the compass the right way. Once you have something to work with, or something to work towards, that's when you truly connect with your authentic self, your life and the world around you. You become the purposeful path that you walk and find excitement in walking the path. You stop obsessing over the destination, or your many goals, and instead focus on the quality you bring to your life through your unique contribution to the world. That's when your why ignites the passion flame within you.

Letting the connection with your why give you direction on where you are heading will also give you focus. It will be easier to say no to things that aren't aligned with who you are, what you stand for, or the kind of positive impact you're looking to create. It will help you create even more positive impact because you will focus all your efforts on embracing this why, hence becoming more efficient and skilful in doing what you do. It also helps you avoid overwhelm and stress as you gain a more balanced control of your passion when you have a clear why that sets the direction for it.

From a psychological perspective, purpose has been sparsely discussed. One of the more popular theories of meaning from W.C. Compton and his colleagues identified purpose, alongside connectedness and growth, as a component of meaning.[51] As you may remember from the first chapter, all of these three elements unlock your inner passion. Having a why and a purpose that is authentic to who you are is the foundation to connecting with your passion energy. Learning and growth, as well as connectedness, not only fuel your passion but also connect you with your sense of purpose (they'll be individually discussed in more depth in Chapter Five and Chapter Six). All of these different elements create a self-reinforcing cycle that you can truly master, and simply tapping into any one of them will help you connect with your passion, which in turn will help reinforce the other elements further.

Another bonus to understanding your why and living life according to it is the associated health benefits. Research has suggested that living a meaningful life through clarity of your purpose improves your mental health and boosts your immune system.[52] It also gives you an improved sense of self-worth and self-confidence, giving you the courage to act authentically throughout your life. This life purpose also gives you a coherent story that helps you connect with your life, and also find the positives in challenging situations.[53] P.A. Boyle and her colleagues' research has gone as far as to suggest that people who have a sense of purpose also live longer and are more likely to be mentally fit for longer.[54]

When it comes to discovering your sense of purpose, it's important for you to be able to separate your past self from the existing self. Even though your past shapes who you are and has a role to play in your story, what you valued and the kind of impact you wanted to create in the past may have changed today. Boniwell and Zimbardo argue that there are three key time perspectives that help fuel your wellbeing and your meaning in life.[55] The first is to find a way to meaningfully connect with your past so you have clarity of your roots and your identity. The second is moderately seeking enjoyment and pleasure in the present so you find a sense of energy that fuels you to act in alignment with your purpose. The third is having a relatively high future orientation so that you have the motivation and drive to work through challenges when you work towards your goals. These three perspectives, connecting the past to the present and the future, ensures your purpose is true to your authentic self, gives you enjoyment as you live your life in alignment with it today, and offers you a direction and focus for the immediate future.

Purpose and Intuition

In his well respected book *Start with Why*,[56] Simon Sinek defines why as the purpose, cause or belief that inspires you to do what you do. He talks about how a why goes a step further than motivation, inspiring you to act with fire and determination rather than you simply doing something for the sake of completing a task. Your why is what gives you a sense of purpose and belonging that is deeply personal to you, and it's often not influenced by external incentives or benefits to be gained. Your why is the belief that sets you in the right direction, your how is the actions you take to realise that belief, and your what are the results of those actions – the positive impact you are creating. Your why is something that feels completely right to you, regardless of what it feels like to others.

This feeling that your why – or even some of your decisions based on your why – is right is often connected with your intuition and gut feeling. When a decision or an action feels right, sometimes we have a hard time explaining the rational thought process behind it. This is because decision making, which is more rational, and your ability to explain those decisions, which is often more connected to your emotional side, are in different parts of your brain.[57] This is why gut decisions, which are connected to your emotions, often feel right. They are controlled by the limbic brain, which also controls our emotions and often knows the right thing to do without being able to verbalise the reasoning.

The reason why the connection with the limbic brain is often referred to as gut feeling is because of the butterflies we feel in our tummy when we make decisions based on it. The limbic brain connects you with the millions of nerve cells in your tummy which results in this feeling of butterflies. This is your subconscious mind telling you something. Psychologists refer to this experience as *"a web of fact and feeling"*.[58] It's this unique web that can also help you to connect with your authentic why.

When you think about your why, try to bring your intuition with you. Some social scientists suggest that the more experienced you are in the domain you're deciding in, or the greater your mastery of it, the more accurate your intuition will be in making the best decision for you.

When it comes to making big life decisions, like discovering the purpose you want to fulfil through your life, your gut feeling is at its most accurate. This is because discovering your why and connecting with it is a highly emotional experience. It is a matter of the heart, not a matter of the rational mind. You can bring in the rational mind later to help you decide how exactly you want to fulfil this life purpose and the actions you need to take to do so, but even then it's important to bring your emotional side with you.

A quote sometimes attributed to Albert Einstein beautifully represents the need for us to stay connected with this intuition perfectly:

> *The intuitive mind is a sacred gift and the rational mind is a faithful servant. We have created a society that honours the servant and has forgotten the gift.*

People who are able to connect with their authentic self will be able to tap into their intuition and as a result connect with a why that's aligned with who they are. These are the people who let their why bring out their most passionate self and live a fulfilling life. These are the people who let their hearts lead the way, but take their rational mind with them on the journey.

Discovering the Why Behind Your Passionate Self
Understanding your why is a lifelong process, and you have the opportunity to start it now. You may already have an idea of what it is, and it could be that you have even experienced a *'eureka moment'*

that connected you with it. One of the participants I interviewed spoke about the moment he clearly understood what his purpose was, and spoke about how everything just fell into place in front of his eyes:

> *I suddenly saw something and it was like all these jigsaw pieces just went click click click click click. And I went, 'Woah that's an art form'.*

The key to discovering your why is testing the waters a lot. It's about action. Why is this? Because only through action do you truly realise how you feel about the idea. You can philosophise, reflect and plan as much as you want, but it's only through doing things that you can truly feel the connection with your why. It's only through testing different approaches that you'll find the meaningful connection to your purpose that you're looking for. In order to understand what action to take, you have some self-studying to do to start brainstorming around your why. We'll start by opening your creativity through connecting with brands, and follow this up with thinking about the legacy you want to leave behind. Last, we'll wrap up by seeing what actions you need to take to connect with your why throughout your life to unlock your inner passion.

1. If I was a brand, which brand would I be and why?

Sometimes it helps to shift the angle from which you look at things. Exploring your why through a branding or marketing perspective can help you identify some of the foundations of your purpose.

EXERCISE:
Identify a maximum of three brands that you connect with. What qualities of these brands do you admire? How would like to portray these qualities yourself through your life?

Think creatively here. The brand could be from any industry and any nation. It could even be someone with a strong personal brand (for example, Steve Jobs). It could be international, or the brand of the local corner kiosk only you and the people in your neighbourhood know. It could be that there is no one brand that you fully, 100%, relate to, but perhaps there are elements of different brands that you find appealing. Don't try to find the 'perfect brand' that is the essence of you (unless you already have one in mind!). Think about how some of your favourite brands communicate their why to you by expressing the qualities that you find appealing.

For example, some of the brands that I really connect with include Apple, Burberry and Innocent. Three completely different brands in completely different industries with completely different target audiences. But there's something about each of them that I really admire and want to portray myself. I love the sleek, simple designs of Apple and that makes me feel good the minute I take whatever Apple device into my hand.

I love the efficient and friendly user experience they've created with every device. When it comes to Burberry, I admire the signature print that stands out from a mile, their effortlessly chic style, and their commitment to staying true to the British origins of the brand. Innocent on the other hand makes me laugh every time I interact with one of their products or social media channels. They are the champions in making people feel good and making people laugh through the little details they have put into their product design (pick up an Innocent smoothie next time you are in town and read the back – you'll know what I'm talking about then!).

These are all qualities I want to portray through myself and my business. Whatever work I deliver through Happyologist and every time I meet someone, I want to make them feel good. I want to leave them better off than when I found them. I want to come across as friendly and I want the work I deliver to be very efficient in delivering the results my clients are looking for. Through Happyologist I've started building a brand that stands out and makes people stop. Equally, I want to stay true to what the Happyologist brand stood for originally, always bringing it back to my authentic self. When I meet people, I want to have a sense of style that feels effortlessly chic, both when it comes to what I wear and how I present myself. At the same time, I also want to have a bit of playfulness and fun through my work and life, being brave enough to laugh at myself when things go wrong or tell funny stories that make me vulnerable.

EXERCISE:
Think about your personal brand. What are the qualities that you want to be known for? What is it that you want people to associate you with?

In a way your why is your personal brand. Think about how you want to come across to people and how that connects you with your why. Think about the role your story has to play in clarifying your why, and how your past shapes the story you have to tell. Reflect on your origins and your roots, and how they've influenced you in wanting to be known for these qualities. Explore each of the qualities in a little bit more depth to see how you'd like to bring these into action in your life. Really look at an ideal scenario here – dream high. Don't limit yourself in what you write as this is really about building the emotional connection. In the third exercise that explores your why we'll start to bring in the rational mind to come up with more actionable outcomes.

Here you might see clear links between your different answers to the first question (the qualities of brands that you admire). In fact, if you find that the qualities are very similar or exactly the same, you already might have a sense of what you want your why to be based on. This is great! Either way, I will give you examples of both situations to help you through the exercise.

So let's say that the qualities you want to be known for aren't necessarily the ones portrayed in the brands mentioned. For me, what I'd definitely like to be known for is an infectious sense of passion and positivity. I'd like for people to connect with me through this passion and positivity, and feel that they have a surge of positive passion energy when they have met me or had a session with me. I also want to be known for how well I connect with people through the messages that I share. I want to share stories and experiences that people can relate to, so that they know we are in this together and we can help each other to live our best, most passionate, happiest lives.

Now let's look at some of the qualities that I mentioned in the first exercise that I definitely want to portray. I definitely want to be known for delivering work that produces results (tying in with the efficiency quality) and also for a sense of fun. This desire to be efficient and deliver results is clearly tied to some of my values, such as the desire to have a sense of achievement and the determination to be of high quality in everything I do. The sense of fun I want to be associated with is more through a positive 'feel-good' factor I want to inspire and encourage, rather than through very expressive extroversion or humour. As a natural introvert, that's something that wouldn't suit me and hence wouldn't work effectively.

From these initial branding exercises you should be able to start to see a common denominator, or at least a few common themes. Keep these in mind as you move on to the next exercise which starts to focus on what kind of positive impact you would like to have.

2. What do I want to create or contribute to that makes the world awesome?

This is your opportunity to really start thinking about the kind of positive impact you want to create. Exploring the kind of contribution you'd like to make to those around you and to the world will give you the foundation to your why. This why will then help you to vocalise a clear purpose to your life and set you in the right direction to living a life a full of passion.

> **EXERCISE:**
> Here it is useful to think about people you admire or people who truly inspire you. What is it about those people that makes them inspirational to you?

When you connect with someone in a way that they become the focus of your admiration or inspiration, you are often connecting through something personal and emotional. You usually don't get inspired by people whose values and aspirations are completely different from yours. You connect with people through something that you both find meaningful. Again, it might be that you connect with only specific qualities of that person, rather than the whole person. These people could be someone in your life, someone from your past, someone you've met once, or people who are well known for what they do. There are no rules here – let your imagination run free and really reflect on the first names that come to your mind.

For example, some of the most inspirational people to me are my mom, my dad, my grandmother, leading positive psychologist Shawn Achor, and my dressage trainer Sarah Millis. These are the people I look up to and their qualities are those that I want to embrace in the way I live my life. My mother raised my three siblings and me as we travelled the world following my father's career. She is the most loving, empathetic, kind person you'll ever meet, and she always goes out of her way to make sure everyone around her is feeling good. My father is one of the most hardworking people I know, and even now in retirement he continues to drive change in the world as he sits on many company boards. His self-discipline and determination to succeed have always been a great inspiration to my three brothers and me. Saying that, his kindness and generosity to help his loved ones in any way possible is also something I am in awe of. Together, my parents are the real power couple.

My grandmother, who is nearly 92 years old now and also known as "Super Mummi" (Finnish for "Super Grandma") to me and my 20+ cousins, is another inspirational icon of hard work, love and wisdom. She patiently and persistently raised eight (eight!!!) children while my grandfather worked hard to provide for the family. She survived World War II and was heavily involved in the rehabilitation of Finland afterwards. Even today she has her own way of creating positive impact as every interaction with her is full of life wisdom and encouragement to be your authentic self.

Shawn Achor is the man who introduced me to the field of positive psychology through *The Happiness*

Advantage (and has since then also released *Before Happiness*[59]). His expertise in the field and his desire to continue researching and exploring new ideas are the kind of qualities I want to always have through my Happyologist work. His vulnerability and how he shows his authentic self in every speaker engagement he does is another powerful reminder to be the real you on whatever stage you are on so people can really connect with your message. Equally, the positive change he creates in the world through the work he does, through sharing his research and through writing these powerful books (both come highly recommended!), is the kind of positive change I want to create through Happyologist, through my research, and through my writings.

Last but not least, my dressage trainer Sarah Millis has truly shown me the meaning of being 'one with the horse'. Her expertise, intuition and love with the horses are breathtaking to watch and every training session I have with her is accompanied by goosebumps. One day I hope to ride even partially as well as she does, but today I already aim for expertise, connectedness with my intuition, and spreading compassion everywhere I go. Her desire to see me succeed as her pupil is also very encouraging and motivating, and always helps me perform. Her belief in my riding capabilities makes me overcome many boundaries and be courageous with the horses. This is how I want to inspire others as well. I want to give my family, friends and clients encouragement, motivation and self-belief too. I want them to be brave and be their authentic selves as that's how they will find their why and fuel their positive passion energy.

EXERCISE:

In ten, forty or fifty years' time, how do you want to be remembered? What is the legacy you want to leave behind?

If you think back to the Alfred Nobel story I shared earlier, you'll recall that he had the opportunity to change his legacy completely in the final years of his life. That is exactly why he is remembered for the Nobel Prizes rather than the invention of dynamite. He was lucky to get that opportunity, and some would even argue that it sounds sad that he only realised in the last decade of his life that the purpose he had been following (playing with inventing explosives) wasn't how he wanted to be remembered. This is why I argue that we should all think about our purpose early on, and adapt it as time moves forward and some life priorities might change. But continuously checking back with your authentic self, and reflecting on that why, will ensure that you are building a life that is aligned with the legacy you want to leave behind.

Now it's your turn to have a go. Imagine that someone was going to make a short speech (anything from a few sentences to a few paragraphs) to celebrate your life at your 80th birthday party. What would you want them to say? Think about all different aspects of your life – from your family to all your social connections to your career to your hobbies and everything in between.

Imagine the ideal scenario – that everything in your life went to plan and you achieved many of your dreams. The closer this speech you write is to your ideal situation, the easier it will be for you to connect with it emotionally, which in turn will shine light on your purpose. Feel free to share the speech with others to show people where you are going, but don't feel obliged to. You might find that if a group of your close connections agrees to complete the exercise, then you can all share it with each other and cheer each other on. But you might also want to keep this completely to yourself, and look at it when you need some inspiration to work towards your why.

EXTRA EXERCISE:
Write about your best possible selves in the future.

Another exercise you may want to try in your own time is writing about your best possible selves.[60] It can help you connect with your authentic self and your values, also shining light on the kind of positive impact you'd like to have in the world. The bonus here is this exercise also boosts your positive emotions and gives you motivation to work towards your ideal scenario. Here are the rules of the exercise:

> - Write for 15 minutes non-stop. Always keep your pen on paper, even writing when you don't know what to write (e.g. *"I'm not sure what to write about*

my ideal self. I already said this and that and I don't quite know what to bring next but...")

- Be as imaginative and creative as you want – do what feels best for you.

- Write however you want but remember to write about imagining your ideal life in the future (you can choose a specific time, for example, in 5/10/15/30 years if you want).

- Do not worry about perfect grammar or spelling, simply keep writing!

- Use as much or as little detail as you want.

- Do this exercise once a week for four weeks, preferably the same day and the same time of the day every week.

Below are the instructions you should read at the start of each session before you start writing. Good luck – and have fun with it!

Take a moment to think about your best possible life in the future (choose a specific year to imagine, e.g., in 10 years' time). Imagine that everything has gone as well as it possibly could. Think about your ideal future in all the different domains of your life (partner, family, career, etc.) and imagine that you are living the best possible life that you could have ever hoped for.

Now, for the next 15 minutes, write about what you imagined.

Once you've completed this exercise over four weeks, think about what it taught you about yourself and what you want from life. Explore how what you imagined could connect you with your purpose in life.

3. How can I practically embed this why into my daily life?

Now that you have explored the qualities that you want to portray and the legacy you want to leave behind, you should have a clearer sense of the kind of positive impact you want to create. With that in mind, I'd like you to have a go at writing down one to two sentences that represent your purpose.

For example:

> *My purpose in life is to inspire, encourage and educate people to help them live lives full of passion, happiness and fulfilment. I want to help people understand how they can choose to be passionate, happy and fulfilled in their life, and how to use this understanding to fulfil their potential and be successful.*

Now it's your turn – write it down below. And if you think you have a few whys, try to add them too in a shortened version (e.g., if you're a parent it's likely one of your whys or your overarching why has a very specific connection to your children or being a parent).

You can start it however you want. Some examples of what you could start with are *"My purpose in life is…"*,

"The why behind what I do is…", or *"The positive impact I want to create is…"*.

> **EXERCISE:**
> *Write down your purpose below:*

Next it's time to reflect on how you are already living this purpose in your life.

> **EXERCISE:**
> Start by reflecting on how you are already living this why. What components of your life are helping you fulfil this why?

Connecting your why to your existing life is the best way to create an immediate positivity boost and start unlocking the inner passion energy without changing a thing. A lot of the passion energy comes from self-awareness, and creating meaningful connections in your existing life helps you to light that fire right away without any excuses. This lays the foundation to your why as it shows how you are naturally, subconsciously already connected to it in one way or another. Really think hard here and don't leave this exercise without having written down at least five things in your existing life that already connect you to your why. For example, they could be specific activities, how you make decisions, or how you interact with people. Or maybe it's something you do that helps inspire others to behave in a way that's aligned with your why. Really think out of the box here.

Before I concretely pinpointed what my why was, I was surprised to find how many things in my life were already connected to it. In a way, my purpose had crept in from the subconscious into certain aspects of my life. Realising this made me feel even more sure of this purpose and gave me the confidence to let this purpose set the direction in my future life. Just to give you an example, here are the five things that I realised connected me to my why in my corporate life:

> - What I enjoyed most about my corporate role was all the social media interaction and blogging I got to do because every tweet or post was an opportunity to leave people better off than when I found them.
> - I was always looking for ways to spread positivity and fun in my corporate office, like bringing in Scandinavian treats for the team to enjoy and doing a 'Lego challenge' with the team.
> - I was involved in a lot of networks and meet ups that were all about sharing knowledge and helping each other grow. In a way, I was already very involved in helping people fulfil their potential.

- I made time to train and compete with my horse, which is a big part of bringing me joy and helping me connect with my authentic self. Simply doing this and talking about it openly often inspired others to make time for things they enjoyed.

- I ran a personal blog in which I shared some of my favourite experiences and stories in an attempt to spread positive energy.

EXTRA EXERCISE:
Draw a Purpose Pie.

Another exercise to help you reflect on this would be to draw a pie with different slices, each slice representing a domain of your life that's very important to you. The number of slices can be as little or as many as you want though sticking to a number between five and eight is recommended to create balance yet avoid overwhelm. You can name your slices whatever you want as long as you know what they mean to you.

Then score yourself on each slice to see how satisfied you are with how well you think that specific life domain currently reflects your purpose (0 being not satisfied at all and 10 being extremely satisfied). It's important to jot down one or two notes explaining why you've given that score for that area of your life, and also to be clear about how this area reflects your purpose (or how you'd like it to reflect your purpose). It's completely fine for different areas of your life to reflect your purpose more than others as long as that is how you want it to be. Just be aware of this and how it might shift the balance in your life, as those with a clear alignment with your purpose will be easier to navigate as you have a core direction you're heading in.

I've sketched an example of a Purpose Pie below, which shows what it could look like.

EXERCISE:
What could you do daily to connect with your why?

Finding new ways to connect with your why will enable you to keep that passion energy running throughout the whole day and across your different life domains. You will have more clarity on the direction you're heading in, and hence make future decisions that will adapt your life to one that helps you to fully embrace that why. This is another question where the Cheat Sheet (page 233) in the back of the book can prove to be useful.

Referring back to your answers from the previous exercise, think about how you're already living your why in your different life domains and which of your life domains you'd like to incorporate more of your why in. Creating meaningful connections with different things in your life will make you much more fulfilled, efficient and proactive in general because you will care about the things you are committing to. You will care because you will understand the purpose behind them, and hence feel authentically connected to them. This in turn will bring that passion out of you and even further fuel your drive to fully live your why.

EXTRA EXERCISE:
Think about how you can incorporate your why into your daily habits.

Here are some questions to consider when you're thinking about how to better incorporate your why into your daily habits:

- Is there something in your life that you're doing that already reflects your why that you would like to do more of?
- In which area of your life would you like to express more of your why? How will you do this, and when will you start doing this?
- What is one action that you can take today that will help you to connect with your why?
- How could you remind yourself daily to connect with your why?
- What is one habit that you'd like to introduce that would help you connect with your why daily?
- Is there something that is preventing you from fully embracing your why? How could you stop this from happening? Could you replace this 'barrier' with something that would help you live your why instead?

Maybe even your key chain, a charm on your bracelet, or the image on your computer could be a daily reminder of your why (the bracelet worked for me!). The key here is to also incorporate actions for you to live your why better. For example, I set up a blog and a weekly newsletter to give tips to the world on how to live their most passionate, happiest lives. I started to smile more in public transport (yes, I'm the weirdo who tries to be friendly on the underground!). I started to do more personal development aligned with my purpose, reading all kinds of books, blogs and magazines in positive psychology.

With every action I took I felt closer to my purpose, yet I felt the career that I had working in corporate marketing didn't enable me to fully embrace it. After this realisation I understood I wanted to commit my whole career to focus on this. This is when I decided to do my Master's in Applied Positive Psychology to specialise in the field and to set up my Happyologist business. Today, I get to coach, train and offer talks every day to help individuals, teams and organisations to fulfil their potential. I decided to shake up my life quite drastically from a comfortable, corporate position to a very new, uncertain entrepreneurial role but I felt this was the most authentic way to connect with my why. And today I'm very happy I had the courage to do this as I'm feeling more passionate than ever.

That doesn't mean that you need to change your career or some key aspect of your life to fully embrace your why – unless you want to. I had a clear vision of what I realised I wanted, and hence I set myself on a path to achieve it. Equally, I could have happily stayed in the corporate world and tried to modify my position, or change positions within the company, to better connect with my why. Sometimes it's as simple as having a conversation with your manager to see if there are some potential new projects on the table. Really consider all options before making any drastic decisions, and always keep your authentic self and your overarching why at the heart of every decision.

Live Your Why
These exercises and questions will help you light the fire within you and give you the confidence to act on

things. Now, having explored your answers, you should have a clearer idea of the kind of positive impact you want to create. You can see the bigger picture and how you're already contributing to the world, as well as what you'd like to do more of to connect with your purpose in a more holistic way. To stay in touch with this why, keep these three points in mind:

1. You can have any type of 'why' you want. Having purpose doesn't mean you need to be curing cancer or negotiating for world peace. As long as you understand the purpose behind your actions and the impact you are looking to create, you have a 'why'.

2. When you are trying to identify the current purpose behind what you do, think about the legacy you are looking to leave behind. How is it that you want to be remembered? Don't judge what you write down but embrace it. Ignore what society says about how you should be remembered but think about how YOU want your friends and family to remember you.

3. The clearer you are about your current purpose, the easier it will be for you to make important decisions when it comes to your lifestyle and career. This in turn will help you take your passion with you wherever you go because you will always understand the why behind what you do.

Remember to keep this why aligned with your values and who you are, because that is the only way it unlocks your positive passion energy and helps you to live your best possible life.

Don't worry about what the world needs. Ask what makes you come alive and do that, because what the world needs is people who have come alive.
~ Howard Thurman ~

five

Master the Art of Learning

*Live as if you were to die tomorrow. Learn
as if you were to live forever.*
~ Mahatma Gandhi ~

The third element that is key in bringing out your inner passion is about seizing every opportunity to learn and grow. When you embark on new adventures that develop your skills and your authentic self, you connect with your passion and fuel the energy it provides. Learning also connects you further with your purpose, especially because everything you learn you can use to create more positive impact around you. This is why living your whole life with passion is a self-reinforcing spiral. The different elements that unlock your passion further fuel each other and the passion that you find within.

Committing to your very own personal development journey is one of the biggest gifts you can give to the world. The more you develop yourself, the more you are able to help the world progress, and the more people you will touch with your unique purpose. The more you invest in your growth, the more you'll encourage the people around you to grow with you. Entrepreneur Jim Rohn expresses this beautifully:

> *The greatest gift you can give somebody is your own personal development. I used to say, 'If you will take care of me, I will take care of you.' Now I say, 'I will take care of me for you, if you will take care of you for me'.*

It's only by investing in your own growth and development that you can truly connect with your potential, as well as with the potential of the world. Mastering the art of learning will help you to find new, exciting ways to approach things, make you more open to facing challenges, help you spot unique opportunities around you, and teach you to use failure as fuel for growth. This in turn will not only unlock your inner passion, but also bring more daily joy into your life. Research has repeatedly shown that you are at your happiest when you are growing.[61] It's this sense of moving forward, becoming the best version of you that you can be, and fulfilling your potential that make you feel good when you know you are learning something new.

This is your opportunity to truly take control of your learning and growth, and invest in it like never before. Master the things that are important to you, use your growth to create more positive impact in new ways, and get ready to face every challenge with hunger rather than fear. Connect with your authentic self, and with your purpose, and you'll naturally start to spot those opportunities for learning all around you.

Learning and Passion

Embracing learning in new, creative ways throughout your life help connect you to your passion and find fulfilment. Some assume that the education system is responsible for giving us new knowledge and enhancing our growth. In reality, the education system and other formal qualifications are only one tiny component of learning. You have the opportunity to learn and grow in everything you do, from the most efficient way to brush your teeth to the most appealing way to present a campaign to developing your fitness to run a mile. You have the choice to actively seek skill development and learning in everything you do, and the more you do, the more you'll fuel the positive passion energy within you.

The people I interviewed about passion spoke about learning and growth in many different lights:

> - *"Through finding something I wanted to pursue and doing it, it's like I've learned a lot more about what's possible".*
> - *"You get drawn into this topic, and then you start understanding more and more and then you kind of, it opens more worlds".*
> - *"It's probably quite ironic now that I'm looking at new areas but maybe that's just something about staying fresh or, you know, keeping things moving".*

They spoke about how once they were in touch with their authentic self and had a sense of purpose, they connected with learning in a new way. It helped them realise the real magnitude of what was possible, opening their eyes to new kinds of opportunities that they weren't able to see before. They spoke about how the more they immersed themselves in learning about something, the more excited they got about it and the more it offered them new perspectives. Some of them questioned themselves when they wanted to learn things in 'new areas' but at the same time they felt it gave them a sense that they were moving forward.

This is one of the hidden secrets of learning. The more you engage in new activities or enhance your skills in ways that are completely different from your usual approach, the more you will actually develop and grow in your usual areas as well. Learning something completely new builds new neural pathways in your brain, which means that you are starting to use more of your brain's capacity. This ability to develop your brain whenever something new is learned or memorised is called *neuroplasticity*.[62] The research around this has shown how your skills and behaviours can be developed, and how what you learn affects different areas of your brain.

It is easiest to activate the learning centres in your brain when you are feeling positive. When you find joy your brain releases the feel-good hormones serotonin and dopamine, which activate the learning centres of our brain.[63] This in turn improves your awareness, focus and detail orientation. In a way embracing your growth journey is about being able to connect with the present, and be in the 'here and now'. When you are mindful of where you are, you are more aware of your thoughts and behaviours. This in turn will help you to spot new opportunities to grow, and also notice the growth as it happens within you.

As you learn to notice the growth that happens within you, you will also see the positive effects the learning has on your happiness and wellbeing. Learning exposes you to new ideas and adventures, letting you enjoy all kinds of experiences you might not do if you weren't committed to developing yourself. It helps you to stay curious and engaged, and fuel the excitement you feel for the everyday. As you notice your personal development, you get a sense of progress and fulfilment which feeds a sense of accomplishment. This also boosts your self-confidence and resilience: you believe that you are capable of overcoming challenges because you are capable of learning how to overcome then.

Learning about different things keeps your brain in shape, just like exercising and healthy nutrition keep your body in shape. Studies have shown that the more active you keep your brain, the less likely you are to suffer from mental illnesses like Alzheimer's disease at a later date.[64] Learning has the power to connect you with yourself, your purpose and your inner passion because you can focus your learning around these things. You can learn about your values, how to better live them, and how to develop the confidence to take them wherever you go. You can learn about what kind of positive impact you want to create, the purpose you want to live your life by, and the ways you want to live this purpose. Simply by picking up this book you've chosen to learn about connecting with the positive passion energy that has the power to fuel your happiness, fulfilment and performance.

Henry Ford described learning beautifully as a way to stay young: *"Anyone who stops learning is old, whether at twenty or eighty. Anyone who keeps learning stays young. The greatest thing in life is to keep your mind young."* In fact research has shown how elderly people who commit to reading, interacting with people, playing games and learning new things keep their brains healthier longer. They are less likely to suffer from Alzheimer's and dementia because they have made a commitment to keeping their brain in shape by continuing to learn.[65]

Acquiring new knowledge is only the first step in learning. The real magic happens when you put your learning into action. Also be open minded to how you can learn, or who you can learn from. Reading, inspirational talks and documentaries might be the obvious choice – but go a step further into experiential learning. What about trying a new sport, doing a drawing class, or joining your local theatre group? Getting involved in things completely unknown to you can offer you all kinds of new insights and perspectives in life. Thinking about what you liked about them and didn't like about them can also help you learn more about yourself, and potentially inspire you to bring new, exciting activities into your life. Have a go at exploring things that really push you out of your comfort zone as these are the things most likely to help you grow, and give you a real sense of accomplishment as you get involved in them.

The last point to mention about learning and passion is that they both happen consciously and subconsciously. You can engage in deliberate practice to improve in something specific, and hence you develop your conscious competence in it. What we sometimes forget is that our minds are processing new information and learning from the things around us without us necessarily being aware of it at that time. Your brain has the capacity to process only 40 bits of information every second.[66] That means you are consciously aware of 0.0000036% of the eleven million pieces of information that your senses are receiving. That means that your body or intuition could be collecting information into your subconscious that your brain isn't actively aware of in that moment. The lesson here is that the more you focus your attention on seeking learning, the more aware of it you will be, and hence the more you will be able to benefit from it.

There is a clear learning spiral happening through all these different elements. The more positive you are, the more in touch with your learning you will be. The more you learn, the more you'll connect with yourself. The more aware you are of your authenticity, the easier it will be to spot opportunities to learn that help you live your purpose. The more you connect with your purpose, the more you'll strengthen the bond you have with your passion.

Adopting a Growth Mindset

In order to truly commit to your learning journey, it is important that you learn to embrace what psychologists call a *growth mindset*. Before I explain to you what that is, let me ask a question. Do you believe that your traits and skills are permanently fixed? Or do you believe they can be developed? This is the underlying belief that sets the foundation to your learning journey which helps you connect with your inner passion. Research has shown that if you believe that you can develop your skills or traits, you can improve anything from your IQ to your emotional intelligence to being more extroverted if you wanted to.[67] Adopting a growth mindset means that you believe that your traits and behaviours are flexible so you can always work on developing them.[68]

Changing your fixed mindset (the belief that your traits and behaviours are fixed and unchangeable) to a growth mindset has numerous benefits. You will appreciate yourself more, which in turn will boost your performance. You will learn and grow more because you will be actively seeking new opportunities to grow. You will find more enjoyment in the things you do because you will see them as learning opportunities which unlock your passion. All of these in turn will fuel your positive emotions and sense of meaning as you will be closer to fulfilling your potential as someone who is on an ongoing personal development journey.

The first step to connecting with your passion through a growth mindset is acknowledging that you would like to adopt it. The next is about becoming aware of your thoughts, because it is the fixed mindset thoughts which often creep in from your subconscious to cloud your mind and prevent you from taking on new challenges to learn. Carol Dweck highlights some of the most common thoughts which take over your mind in her brilliant book *Mindset,* and explains how to overcome them so you can truly embrace learning.

1. *"I can't develop my skills in this."*
   Believing that you can't develop your skills in a particular area or activity is fixed mindset thinking. Whatever it is, you can always learn to do something better, even if it's simply about learning to do it differently or more efficiently. The question you need to ask yourself is how developing this particular skill could enhance your life or career, or help you create more positive impact. When you understand the why behind it, and believe that growth is possible, you're much more likely to commit to developing.

2. *"I can't do this because I need to be perceived as [smart] and this wouldn't be aligned with other people's perceptions of me."*
   This goes back to the first key element of pursuing your whole life with passion: being authentic. The thoughts of others shouldn't matter, especially because you can never control them. You need to embrace the real you, be comfortable with that, and focus on developing your real self to your benefit and the benefit of the world.

3. *"I'm not taking on that challenge because I don't want to fail."*

Take up challenges as an opportunity to learn. If you never fail, you're less likely to learn. So take risks, look for challenges and try things differently. I guarantee you'll discover some real, unexpected gems in taking on challenges, and you'll be more likely to succeed. You'll also have a hell lot more fun embracing all kinds of adventures!

4. *"I'm giving up before I even start because I don't believe I'm capable of getting through the challenge."*

Fixed mindset thinking makes you give up easily. When you are connected with your authentic self and have a clear idea of your purpose, you will find it easier to embrace your growth mindset. You will persist at things because you know they matter to you, and you will see obstacles as something that motivates you to keep going further.

5. *"Talented people don't need to put any effort in, they are naturally good at everything."*

This belief cannot get any more 'fixed mindset' if it could. Fixed mindset people think that effort is something that only untalented people have to put in. Growth mindset on the other hand sees effort and hard work as something that will get you where you want to go. Put the hard work in, and you'll find that success tastes so much sweeter too.

6. *"I feel so threatened by her success."*
   Use other people's success as inspiration for you to succeed. Focus on what you could learn from them, and talk to them about what they think the secrets behind their success are. Learn from their learnings.

7. *"I'm not taking on board that feedback because it makes me feel bad."*
   I say ignore the criticism but take on the constructive feedback. Useful feedback will help you to develop, grow and move forward towards your goals. Your family, friends, colleagues and clients want to help you to improve, so listen to the constructive feedback they give to you.

This can seem like an overwhelming list of things to think about but in essence it's all about becoming more aware of your thoughts and how you approach learning. The more awareness you build, the easier it will be for you to challenge your fixed mindset thoughts, and change them into growth mindset ones. The more of a growth mindset you adopt, the more you'll embrace learning, and the easier it will be to connect with your passion energy. I can confess that this might not be easy for you, but this is when the saying, 'Most things worth having don't come easy', has some truth.

After years of practising this myself, I still find myself having fixed mindset thoughts but I now find it easier and quicker to change them into growth mindset ones. At the same time, you can listen to Shakespeare's wisdom too, and realise that it's only difficult if you choose to think of it in that way: *"For there is nothing either good or bad, but thinking makes it so."* Learn to adopt a growth mindset and you'll see the challenges that lie ahead in a much more positive light. See the growth mindset as a key ingredient to connecting with your learning journey, and find more fulfilment in your day to day.

Aiming for Mastery in Life

One of the other elements which tie learning, passion and the growth mindset together is the desire for mastery. Often mastery is referred to as comprehensive knowledge or expert skill in a specific subject or activity. What I'm suggesting here is to aim for mastery in life overall. This doesn't mean that you become the expert of everything you do, but that you become the best version of you that you can be in everything you do. That you are always aiming to improve yourself, to develop and to grow in the different activities in your life. That you learn to master your own life.

Mastery might mean different things to you, especially in different domains in your life. The focus might be on specific areas, and these often fluctuate throughout your life. For example, if you're not really into cooking, you want to master creating nutritious, yummy meals quickly. If you want to work on speaking up more in the workplace, you want to master your confidence to contribute in departmental meetings when you do have something to say. If you want to build a life that's financially viable in the long term, you want to master personal money management, which could cover anything from staying on top of your spending to saving to pension plans and more. The key is that you understand how you want to master the different domains in your life that are important to you.

When you allow yourself to fully get immersed in different activities in order to learn, you have a high likelihood of experiencing flow. Mihaly Csikszentmihalyi refers to flow as "the psychology of optimal experience" and defines it as a mental state in which you are fully immersed in energised focus, full involvement and enjoyment when you are engaged in a specific activity.[69] Flow most often occurs when you are engaged in something that is highly challenging and involves a high level of your skills that you are confident you have or can start to develop then and there. This is why it is so common to experience flow in learning experiences, especially when you are learning something that you are really interested in and already quite highly skilled in.

Many experiences of flow can be seen as experiences that connect you with a sense of mastery because you are engaged in something that you value, are relatively highly skilled in, and are being asked to grow in doing it. Hence it is taking you one step closer to mastering that particular activity. Experiencing flow also helps you to connect with your inner passion because through it you are allowing yourself to get fully immersed in activities that are connected with your authentic self. Because flow is most often experienced in things you enjoy and are intrinsically motivated to do, flow also fuels the passion energy that comes from doing things aligned with your true self and your authentic purpose.

One of the key drivers of mastery is to master living your authentic purpose. When you commit to learning and growing, you are always looking for ways to improve who you are and how you can better deliver the positive impact you want to deliver. Commit to mastering your life, your purpose and your passion, and you will feel those learnings light up your positive energy within.

Embracing Passionate Learning

Learning has the opportunity to follow you everywhere if you choose to acknowledge it and embrace it. You can commit to lifelong learning and live a more adventurous, exciting life that's full of surprising joys, moments of fulfilment and passion. In order to connect with your learning self, I have outlined three sets of exercises below. The first of these asks you to explore your current experiences of learning and how you view them. The second is about learning to embrace the growth mindset, which is a key ingredient in fulfilling your learning potential. The third, and final one, encourages you to identify new learning opportunities you can commit to from tomorrow onwards.

1. How does learning enhance my life?

The first step in embarking on a new, more fulfilling learning adventure is to acknowledge how it already exists in your current life. This is an exercise that will help you become more self-aware and appreciate how learning has shaped your life so far.

> **EXERCISE:**
> How do you feel when you are learning something new, or after you have learnt something new?

Here I'm asking you to connect with your emotions again. This keeps recurring because in order for you to be fully aware of your authentic self and to meaningfully connect with the passion within you, you need to be in touch with your emotions. Think about what goes on in your head and heart when you are experiencing something new, or when you are actively choosing to develop your skills in something. Think about both the conscious element, by reflecting on how you feel when you are learning, and the subconscious element, by thinking about how you feel after you've learned something new.

For example, every training session I have with my horse teaches me something new. My trainer, who has the wealth and knowledge of being a professional dressage rider for more than 15 years, pushes my horse and me out of our comfort zone in every training session. We are both working hard mentally and physically to achieve what she asks of us. I usually get very involved in the moment and I'm very focused and reflective. When I finally connect with what she's trying to get me to do, and my horse responds in the way that we want, I feel very intense euphoria. I feel in perfect harmony with the horse, and time stops as I become one with him. The joy I feel is indescribable and my self-confidence shoots sharply up. This could be described as experiencing flow, especially because I am looking to master my riding and after 18 years of doing it I'm already quite highly skilled in it. This feeling of joy is accompanied by an immense sense of accomplishment and I am on a high pretty much for the rest of the day.

Another example is of a time I tried something completely different and new. My family and I organised a day full of activities for my father's 60th birthday. One of the activities was something that none of us had tried before: curling. Having seen it on television before (and never been too interested in it), I was surprised to discover how difficult it was. The amount of muscle strength, coordination and accuracy needed to push the stone successfully was a huge surprise, and that was on top of the mental focus which was necessary to complement the accuracy of my body coordination. Needless to say, the results varied massively! I gained a whole new sense of appreciation for the sport and see it from a completely new perspective now. I enjoyed the learning process because it was one way to have fun with my family. We cheered each other on and laughed a lot (especially when it came to the 'sweeping the ice' bit on front of the stone). It reminded me of the importance of trying completely new things. I felt energised, giggly and creative afterwards. I wanted to go find out more about the sport and do it again just for fun. I also realised how fun it is to learn something new with family or friends – it's a great bonding experience and when everyone is a newbie it can be a really good laugh!

> **EXERCISE:**
> How has learning benefitted you or those around you in the past? Be specific and use concrete examples when you answer this question.

I want you to answer this going beyond the points that I've already made. Yes, it fuels your happiness, your fulfilment and your passion. Yes, it helps you grow and develop. And this all in theory makes the world progress. But I want you to get more specific than that. I want you to think of specific examples of how learning has helped you in the past.

Perhaps a specific learning has helped you to reach a specific goal, or to change careers. Or perhaps trying something new with your partner helped fuel their happiness. Maybe some learning brought you closer to a family member you'd lost touch with, or maybe it helped you realise how you wanted to change your life. Try to avoid general answers like *"It helped me progress in my career"*; go very deep and specific instead: *"Learning how to influence people has helped me to negotiate better deals with clients, to secure the sales manager role and to help my family shift into a positive mood on a rough day."*

For example, I have found that learning about different tools in positive psychology has helped me build the ideal life for me. All the tools I have learned from my studies and work I use on myself. It has given me a new sense of self-awareness, connected me with my authentic self, and made me feel that I am enough just the way I am. The first tool that started this learning experience for me was the 'Three good things' exercise (described below).

EXTRA EXERCISE:
Finish every day by writing down three things you are grateful for.

I did this exercise for 21 days in a row, and realised a complete mind shift was starting to happen. This was a real eye opener for me, and was my first connection to positive psychology. This little learning made me realise I wanted to work in this field and help people find happiness. This little learning led me to discover my purpose.

The best part about having studied positive psychology means that I can inspire and encourage people around me with the knowledge I have of it. The learnings I have had by doing my own positive psychology interventions on myself means I've experienced the change myself and can share these stories with the people I connect with to help them have their own, unique positive experiences. For example, learning about the growth mindset was a real epiphany for me and I have done my best to share the idea behind it with anyone

I've come across who I thought would find it interesting and useful in their lives.

I can remember one specific instance in a client social event I had been invited to attend. I was explaining what I do with my clients to a new acquaintance and he was intrigued by some of the happiness concepts I shared with him. He went on to say, *"I feel like I've reached my potential, overcome all my odds, and I just think I should settle here because I'm not smart enough to progress any further in my career"*. Just hearing this was quite a shock to me as it's such a negative self-belief to hold about yourself. I asked him some of the fixed mindset and growth mindset questions, to identify which mindset was closest to his, and then I challenged him on some of his beliefs. One of the questions I saw make an impact was, *"5 years ago did you think you'd get to where you are today?"*. He said *"no, not really"*, so that was my argument to him to now also imagine that in five years he could be somewhere where he right now thought was nearly impossible. I used a few coaching questions to provoke his thinking and introduce the growth mindset ideas. He definitely didn't buy in to them then and there but he admitted he had some things to think about and he thanked me for the time I'd given to talk to him about this.

This is only one example of many when I've taken one of my most impactful learnings and shared it with someone else in the hopes of helping them out. In that way, learnings not only help me grow, develop and find happiness and meaning, but also help inspire and encourage others to do the same. Not only do I do this in personal interactions, through the work I do with my clients, but also through my social media channels and through my Happyologist.co.uk blog which has a very supportive, loyal following made up of people who are amazing at appreciating the learnings I share with them.

2. How could I better adopt a growth mindset throughout my life?

If you choose to adopt a growth mindset, you become a more malleable individual. You realise that you can improve yourself in any area you want, and believe that you are a dynamic individual always developing and growing. These two questions will help you to start embracing the growth mindset by looking at a past experience when it was nowhere to be seen, and by looking at how you can position failure as something positive.

> **EXERCISE:**
> Think of a time you faced a challenge and you heard the 'fixed mindset voice' saying you didn't believe you could overcome the challenge. How could you have talked back to it with a growth mindset voice or taken a growth mindset action?

You often don't hear the fixed mindset thinking when it shoots up from your subconscious because you are so focused on the challenge itself. Focusing on the challenge in hand can make you more and more negative about it if you simply look at how difficult it will be to overcome. You shut down your positivity and disconnect from the learning centres in your brain. This subconscious mind comes through with fixed mindset thoughts like, *"I can't do this"*, *"This is too difficult for me"*, and *"I've never done something like this before so that means I'm not capable of doing anything like this."* This is when you need to become more self-aware of your thoughts so that you can challenge them and replace them with more positive ones that motivate and encourage you.

The fixed mindset voice can come to you in many different instances, from situations with your family to issues at work to physical challenges. I remember not getting a distinction in my first assignment in my Master's (yes, as an ambitious perfectionist I was a bit of nerd with high expectations of myself in class). Immediately the fixed mindset voice came loud and clear saying, *"You're stupid"*, *"You didn't work hard enough"*, and *"You can never enter the field if you can't even get a distinction on a silly assignment"*. Luckily, I had personally just learned about the growth mindset and I quickly replaced these negative reflections with growth mindset thoughts: *"This is the first scientific paper I've ever written, I can learn how to do it better"*, *"A grade of one academic assignment does not reflect my intelligence"*, and *"This is a great learning experience about putting the growth mindset into action."*

Another challenge I faced that had many fixed mindset voices battling with it continuously was publishing this book that is in your hands right now! Originally I thought I couldn't publish a book because I didn't have a PhD, because no one had approached me to ask me to write a book, and because I had never done it before (yes, a bit of a catch 22 there!). It was through talking to some of the close people around me I was able to embrace the idea with a growth mindset, and I got the confidence to start planning for it. Within one month I had a book proposal in my hands. Within two months I had put the first words on paper. Within three months I had written 75% of the book. Throughout the process the fixed mindset kept coming back to me saying things like, *"No one will read your book because you don't run a big company like Apple or Starbucks"*, or *"You can't self-publish because you don't know anything about publishing."* I overcame those thoughts by writing a sales pitch about my book and telling practically everyone I met about it. (I owe a special thanks to the people who received my book pitch with great enthusiasm and excitement – it's their positive energy that gave me the courage to keep going!). I did lots of online research about self-publishing, started talking to freelance editors, and found out how the process worked. And voilà, here is the book in your hands – and I still can't believe it's true!

EXERCISE:
When was the last time you experienced a massive failure? Explore what you learned from the experience and how it changed you.

Failure is a big word in our society and we are subject to it at an early age in the education system when we can potentially 'fail' assignments or classes if we don't perform as well as what is considered the norm. 'Failing' continues to be a very negative word in the business world and is often seen as unacceptable. This societal belief makes it difficult for us to challenge ourselves, push boundaries and try new things because we are afraid that if we fail we will be punished or laughed at. Luckily this belief is getting challenged more and more, especially in the business world where it prevents creativity and innovation. Now it's time you explored the idea of seeing failure as a learning experience, not as "*lack of success*", "*nonperformance*", or "*insufficiency*" (as defined by dictionary.com).

This massive failure could be in any context or of any magnitude. Even though it might seem minuscule to someone else, it's perfectly ok for it to feel massive to you. I challenge you to pick something that you haven't seen as a learning experience before. I want you to pick something that really made your heart drop and made you question yourself, even if only for a second. I'll do the same right now right here with you.

For me, something I experienced as a massive failure was not getting my research paper about the passionate way of being published in my number one journal choice. I had selected it specifically because I knew the audience would be the type of audience interested in my study yet I knew that they rarely (if ever) published papers based on qualitative research. The journal also had a very high impact factor, and as someone without a PhD or professional doctorate it was quite a stretch for me to even apply. Knowing all that, however, didn't make it easier to deal with the 'failure'. I was frustrated as I felt they were holding me back from sharing my knowledge with the world. I was disappointed because I felt that they were somehow rejecting me or the massive amount of work I had put into the research paper. I took it a little too personally.

So what did I actually learn from it? I learned to not take things personally! I understood that the academic game is a different one from the business one I'd been playing for years, and that I had not yet learned to play it. I learned that what you think is an ideal match isn't always the case. I learned that sometimes a reality check is useful before committing a lot of time and energy towards a goal that had no real meaning behind it. Originally, I simply wanted to ensure the paper got published so the world would know about it, yet I gained this obsessive idea that it had to be in this journal because the journal title had "happiness" in it. I learned that sometimes you have to ask yourself why you have set yourself this goal, and challenge the reasoning behind it.

How did it change me? It made me more aware of the things I needed to work on – craving recognition externally, feeling a higher sense of achievement if I published in a bigger name journal or worked with big name clients, and setting goals without a clear why. Today I find a daily sense of achievement by finishing the day by looking at everything I've accomplished. I have a success file on my computer full of positive feedback from present and previous clients, my blog followers, and family and friends. I look at it whenever I need to be reminded that I'm doing exactly what I want to be doing and that I'm actually good at it. Saying that, I believe that you can always be better, no matter what, and that's why ongoing learning is so important.

3. Where in my life and career do I have opportunities to learn more?

We are all trying to make the best of our time on Earth every day (with a select few doing the same in outer space these days!). Sometimes we get so sucked into our work, life and routines that we forget to invest in our own development. Other times we think that we are already an expert in what we do so there's no need to keep learning. Both of these are very dangerous pitfalls. If we overcome the first we can actually habitualise learning and development which will make us more passionate, happier and more likely to reach our full potential.

We need to overcome the second pitfall to action the first one. In the words of Denis Waitley, *"Never become so much of an expert that you stop gaining expertise. View life as a continuous learning experience."* You might be specialised in a specific area or industry, or maybe you've mastered a specific art form or sport. You might even market yourself as an expert to sell your services. But that absolutely does not mean that you are finished with learning. The minute you stop learning is the minute you stop succeeding. Life is dynamic and the world is continuously evolving around you, so you need to stay on the lifelong learning journey to make the most of it.

> **EXERCISE:**
> List at least 10 things you could do to learn more in your life.

This is a good time for you to pause and think about how you could connect with your learning self in a better way. Remember, it will not only help you learn new skills, try new activities, and help you move towards your goals – it will also fuel your passion, positivity and performance. Really think about how these 10 things that you identify could enhance your development, your life, or the life of others somehow. Again, use the Cheat Sheet at the end of this book to help you if you feel yourself run out of ideas.

I'll go first, as I hope to inspire you with five of the ones on my list:

> - Get a celebration notebook where I write down what I've achieved at the end of every day. It will teach me the habit of celebrating little successes and give me a sense of progress. It will teach me what I'm spending the most time on so I can reflect on whether that is what I want to be spending most of my time on.
> - Read one book a month. I love reading but I never seem to make time for it (I blame Netflix!).

I have a few books on the go now but they have stretched for months so maybe if I committed to one a month I would focus better.

- Get a mentor! I have had different coaches throughout my career and when building up my business, but never a mentor who has been there and done it all. I have connected with many in the field and spoken to them, but it would be amazing to have one go-to person to explore different ideas and concepts with.

- Cook one new dish every fortnight. I'm not big into cooking but when I do cook I always do the same old dishes. Trying a new dish will give me more nutrients and boost my creativity.

- Learn a new make-up look. I'm not big into pampering or doing hair or make-up. This means I'm often with the same signature 'Susanna look' but it wouldn't hurt to try something new every now and then to lift my energies up and enhance my creativity.

If you wanted to take this with a career focus, you could enhance this exercise by listing another five things that are specific to you growing and developing yourself in your work. For example:

- Find a few entrepreneurs to create a 'Business Mastermind Group'. We would meet monthly to share our challenges, successes, failures and best practices with each other to inspire, encourage

and motivate each other. (This is very related to the next chapter on connecting with your tribe!).
- Identify my long-term business goal with the help of my business coach so I can create better focus in my business. I love saying yes whenever there is a client in need but that means sometimes I am doing all kinds of different projects which aren't necessarily helping me grow my business and create the maximum positive impact.
- Take a short online course on neuroscience. What happens in the brain when people are feeling passionate has not yet been researched so I want to understand the basic neuroscience to see if I'd like to explore this in my PhD in the future.
- Review my most popular blog posts and articles online to learn what it is that appeals to people the most. This would educate me on what makes good content and help me create more great content which people would share – hence helping me spread positivity and passion even more.
- Sign-up to the Chartered Institute of Personnel and Development (CIPD) network to connect with other coaching and training professionals. We can share best practices and potentially work together on different projects.

You might be able to spot that all of the learnings on my lists are quite focused but might take a while to complete. Do your lists reflect the same? Remember that the more specific you can be, the easier it will be to achieve that.

You can even try to set a date and time to explore each option, and then create an action plan for each one. In a way, they are mini goals which are helping you grow and develop while helping you live your authentic purpose. The next step is breaking it down into daily actions you can take to keep on learning, be it with the specific approaches above or in any other way.

EXERCISE:
What could you do to commit to growing and developing as a person daily?

Committing to learning and growing daily gives you a sense of adventure and excitement, and connects you with the positive passion energy within. When you find a way to turn learning into a habit, you will naturally be looking for more opportunities to learn and your brain will act like a sponge, sucking all of your learning experiences into your being. At this point you might have your fixed mindset thoughts coming in from the subconscious saying, *"Not one more thing to do!"*, *"I'm too busy to learn"*, or *"I'm too tired to learn"*. The key is to find a way to easily incorporate learning into your existing routine, rather than seeing it as an additional item on your to-do list. See it as a way to make you more productive and to help you perform at your best. See it as something energising and uplifting because that's exactly the way you'll feel.

Of course as with everything the word to keep in mind is *balance*. If you truly invest yourself into the learning world, such as attending a training workshop, committing to a course or doing a full-on accreditation of some sort, you may feel a drop in energy after you've completed it and the high has gone. That's simply your brain digesting all the new learnings and adjusting itself to carry them with you. This is also why it's so important to make learning a part of your daily routine so that it becomes natural to you, rather than something you have to invest extra time and energy into. Perhaps you want to replace an existing bad habit with a more positive habit that boosts learning? Maybe you could approach existing projects or routine tasks with a learning mindset, challenging yourself to do them in a new way?

This is up to you to define but the key is to make it challenging enough so that you push yourself but easy enough so you stay committed to it. For example, every day I get on my horse I say to myself what I am going to be working on (for example, *"I'm going to relax my body so he can relax his"* or *"I'm going to focus on keeping my posture upright and seat still"*). After my work day, I write down my achievements for the day, which teaches me about appreciating the effort I put in, seeing where my focus is and helps me reflect on whether I'm on the right path. When I do laundry, I try different strategies to try and be as efficient as possible in hanging my clothes up to dry (yes, I know it sounds silly but I get creative – and often it's accompanied with some good music and a little boogie). Every day in the evening I read something that teaches me new things – whether it's my latest non-fiction book (often an autobiography or psychology self-help book) or a popular article or blog post online. As I mentioned before, the more specific you can make your new learning habit, the better.

Learn Actively
The day you stop learning is the day you stop succeeding, regardless of how you see success. Always make an effort to put your best self forward to the world by remembering how to embrace your learning self like this:

1. Believe that you can learn and develop in anything you choose to. You are a dynamic individual with incredible potential for growth. The only thing that stands between you and your growth is the belief that you can't grow. So eliminate it right here right now because it's nonsense.
2. Use learning as an excuse to get involved in new, exciting adventures that help you live your life with passion. Don't be afraid to try new things and learn from failures.
3. Think about how you can make sure you're pushing yourself out of your comfort zone every day in a way that's helping you grow and develop in some sense. It's this ongoing journey of learning that will not only keep your passion

flame strong but also give you pleasure, excitement and a sense of achievement.

Not only will this help bring your passion out and keep the excitement of novelty alive, you'll also help the world progress and move forward in your own way. You'll inspire others to bring out their best selves. Best of all, you'll never stop learning because life never stops teaching.

The capacity to learn is a gift;
The ability to learn is a skill;
The willingness to learn is a choice.
~ Brian Herbert ~

six

Connect with Your Tribe

*Only through our connectedness to others can
we really know and enhance the self.*
~ Harriet Lerner ~

The fourth element that unlocks your passion and drives you to live your whole life with passion is connecting with like-minded people. These might be the people you've grown up with, the friends you've chosen to maintain relationships with, the strangers you've connected with in a strange way, or the people who inspire you. These are the people you choose to spend time with because they always leave you feeling better after you've seen or spoken to them. These are the people you actively choose to meet up and connect with rather than the people you are together with because of circumstances (such as work colleagues).

Someone *like-minded* might be someone with similar values, beliefs or ambitions. It could be someone who has had a similar upbringing and understands how that has influenced your rationale for making decisions. Maybe it's someone in a very similar career, or someone who has the same hobby as you. Personally, I also really connect with people who inspire me and those who have a similar why to mine. This is where being aware of your authentic self plays a huge role, because when you understand who you are and truthfully portray it 24/7, only then are you able to create true connections with other people.

These true connections with your tribe will give you a sense of belonging while encouraging you to remain true to who you are. These are the people who openly accept you and your story inside out. These are the people who lift you up when you're down. These are the people who encourage, inspire and motivate you to work hard for your purpose – and you do the same for them. These are the people who help you connect with your true self and with whom you feel confident about being who you are. When you are with these people, you feel at peace with yourself yet excited about what you're working on. Together you bring out the fire from each other. Together you help each other live your best possible lives.

That doesn't mean it's always easy. It's often the people you connect with that give you the most joy as well as the most pain. Sometimes they challenge you to help you progress, or try to push you in a certain direction to help you succeed. Other times they behave in ways which might be hurtful to you but in their eyes they're simply trying to protect you. But these are still the people who are your biggest fans. They are the first ones to celebrate your successes with you and the last ones to question decisions you were confident in making. They are the first ones to help you see failures as learning experiences and the last ones to tell you off for making a mistake.

Connecting with your tribe really helps you connect with your authentic self and your why. It also encourages you to keep on learning and growing, as your tribe is often your biggest inspiration to your learning self. Your tribe is also the one place you know you can go to help reignite your passion if you're feeling the flame is low. Together you unlock each others' positive passion energy within.

Belonging and Passion
When you are surrounded by people who share something with you, be it your values, your beliefs, your why, or something you do together, you feel like you belong. This makes you feel connected and safe. It makes you feel comfortable in your own shoes and you feel confident in being yourself. This desire to belong is a fundamental human need that exists across different cultures. As a human you are naturally driven towards connecting and building long-lasting, positive, significant interpersonal relationships.[70] These relationships evolve past superficial social ties and the meaningful sense of belonging they supply improve your wellbeing.

This desire to belong is basic human biology. Neuroscientists have discovered mirror neurons in the brain which show how we are wired to connect.[71] These specialised cells in the brain generate brain-to-brain links between people, which makes it possible for your brain waves, chemistry and feelings to mirror the brain waves, chemistry and feelings of the person you are talking to.[72] To some extent this brain link can happen even when you're watching or thinking about the people you find fascinating and inspiring because you often instinctively understand their thoughts, feelings, and intentions to some degree.[73] Some scientists argue this is where empathy, and the ability to relate to others, partly comes from, both for ourselves and for others.[74] This is also one of the things that makes passion, as well as emotions and moods, more contagious.

We can unconsciously catch both good and bad moods when we are surrounded by them because we naturally mimic the expressions around us.[75] Studies have suggested it takes as little as one person in a group of five to 'infect' the rest of the group with their mood. Imagine yourself being surrounded by people who are like-minded to you in their values, their why or their desire to be passionate. What do you think the energy would be like in that room? Those mirror neurons could really fire you up as you'd sense positive passion energy even if only a few people had it in the room. This 'infection' is even more powerful when someone you respect and are inspired by, like a leader, walks into the room. Their mood can spread across a room in as little as seven minutes.[76] Now think about a time when you met someone who inspires you or saw them in action (e.g. attended their seminar, saw their TED talk) – how quickly did you feel your energy shift into a more positive place? This is why the tribe you connect with could include friends, family, colleagues, clients and even people who inspire you but with whom you might not even have had a face-to-face interaction yet. If they still have a positive effect on you when you watch them in action, read their articles or tell someone else about them, then they are a good catch. They still have the power to energise you and bring your passion out.

This is exactly what happens when you connect with the people in your tribe. When you feel like you belong you have the confidence to build relationships through trust and build relationships that last. The people you build these relationships with are so passionate and positive about their lives that it rubs off on you. As it rubs off on you, you become more confident in who you are and what you pursue. This confidence in turn fuels that positive passion energy that becomes stronger and stronger the more you use it. That's when you join the self-reinforcing cycle in your tribe, inspiring their passionate selves to come out as they do the same for you. This is the power of the tribe. It brings you together and pushes you forward.

I came across this desire for a sense of belonging in many shapes through my research.

- *"That's quite powerful to be around, a group of 60 people... who are all thinking the same things"*.
- *"There's something about the retreat that brings people together. And ... hearts open up. And people ... share, and they open up, in ways that they can't, or they won't, in their everyday lives"*.

- "It's something I want to do in the community, I think it's a good thing, I like for some other people to join in".

Some reminisced about the strong emotions they felt when they were simply in the presence of like-minded people, and they spoke warmheartedly about the impactful memories they had from spending time with people they could relate to. Others spoke about this desire to create a sense of belonging for themselves and others, for example through retreats and community projects. They described how something unique happens when people come together for similar objectives, and how this togetherness helps people reveal their true selves. Being part of a change process like this which helps others get in touch with their true selves, or creating the environment for it, helped fuel their sense of belonging further.

Someone else spoke about how *"meeting these other inspirational women"* in a female personal development training, and sharing, brainstorming, and discussing with them, helped her think out of the box and get the confidence to keep following her purpose. It helped her step out of her comfort zone and into challenges. It gave her the confidence to be herself which in turn triggered the unlocking of her passion. This is very much in line with the self-determination theory which identifies the ability to relate to others as one of the three key motivational drivers for any behaviour.[77] The other two drivers, autonomy and competence, can also be tied to the unlocking of your passion. Autonomy is referred to as making decisions consistent with the integral self, and hence is very aligned with the idea of being your authentic self. Competence is relevant to both the desire to learn and grow as well as the belief in one's strengths (which will be discussed in the next chapter).

This sense of belonging that you gain from connecting with other like-minded people also leads to feeling valued. The holistic way of feeling valued combines both intrinsic and extrinsic factors, but it is the intrinsic factors that unlock your passion in a positive manner. Sometimes simply being surrounded by like-minded people gives you intrinsic satisfaction as you feel you are in an environment where you are understood and valued for who you are. Other times it is the specific interaction or activities you do with your tribe that also reinforce the idea that you are exactly where you are meant to be, doing exactly what you are meant to be doing. You feel appreciated, connected and at home. Feeling valued through intrinsic satisfaction also comes from being able to feel that what you are investing your time and energy in is valuable and important. Often this can be bound up with the feeling that you are comfortable being who you are and fully committed to your why. The people I interviewed through my research clearly found a sense of belonging and being valued when they felt connected to a greater cause. Some of the comments from the interviewees were:

> - *"It's that it always feels like I'm doing something worthwhile".*

- *"It's very rewarding to ... To take on a big cause, the biggest cause I think that we've ever really faced as human beings".*
- *"I just feel like I'm kind of a channel for some sort of unlocking".*
- *"[They said the event] was meaningful to them, and it changed their life, and it made them rethink about their choices".*

These comments show why you shouldn't underestimate how simply believing in the value that you are creating makes you feel appreciated and like you belong. You can see people felt valued when they felt they were committed to something bigger than themselves, which connects this sense of belonging to the why they live their life by. From Anna's* quote above (the third bullet point), you can see she felt she was a kind of medium to help people get unstuck and release more of what they had in them. She felt confident in the positive effect she had, which played a part in making her feel that the work she was doing was valuable. Conversely, Dan* said how positive feedback (like the one illustrated in the fourth bullet point above) made him feel valued. In my conversations with him he seemed keen for more external recognition, though he admitted over time he has learnt to not rely on it.

This brings me to raise a word of warning on the feedback you get. Yes, it's useful, helpful and makes you feel good, but do not use it as the sole driver of feeling valued. It should be treated as an extra or as a bonus that comes after you've learned to value yourself, your why and how you spend your time. Actively seeking a sense of belonging through extrinsic recognition can lead you to a dangerous path that's not aligned with your authentic self. Instead, it can lead you to a more obsessive path that is defined by what people tell you rather than what you feel is right. The deeper you get into this path, the more you lose control of it, and the harder it is to get out of it.

This is why understanding who is in your tribe is also important. The like-minded people you feel you belong with inspire and encourage you upwards without concretely interfering with how you decide to go about it. They may give you tips and insights when you ask for them, but you need to reconnect with your authentic self before you decide to follow one of their recommendations. Similarly, the people in your tribe who you also inspire and encourage upwards will listen to you if you have feedback, but they are the best people to make the decision on whether this is the right course of action for them.

Simply connecting with your tribe kindles that passion flame inside of you. You know you've found someone who's in your tribe if you feel energised, excited, positive and passionate after you've spoken to them. You might meet them in different places in different scenarios. Some of them you might meet only once, but simply remembering how you felt during that conversation might help you connect with your inner passion. Simply reading about others or hearing their stories might connect you with someone who you might not ever meet but you find inspiration in. This is your tribe so it's your rules. You choose who's in there and who's out. As with everything in life, it might be that some people fuel your passion at certain stages of your life and not so much at others. That's completely normal as your authentic self can change in the different phases of your life and hence you connect with people differently at those different times.

Be open to the people in your tribe because they are all like-minded to you in different ways. Some might spark your passion when it comes to taking care of your body and mind, others might light it up because their why is very aligned with yours. It could also be that you connect with them through a specific value you both have, or through an activity or sport you're both interested in. Your tribe in essence is a mix of different kinds of people that ignite your inner passion in different ways. Marcus Aurelius spoke of this beautifully:

> *When you want to gladden your heart, think of the good qualities of those around you; the energy of one, for instance, the modesty of another, the generosity of a third and some other quality in another.*

However, there is one major common denominator: they accept you for who you are. This brings us back to embracing your authentic self. When you stay in touch with your dynamic authentic self, the why behind what you do, and your learning self, you'll more easily find your tribe and stay connected with the right tribe at the right time. Staying connected with the right tribe will in turn fuel your self-confidence and your belief in your why.

The Dream Tribe

When you find your tribe and make an effort to stay connected with them, you are creating a network of people who are there to push you towards your dreams. Diana Nyad, an open water swimmer who swam from Cuba to Florida at the age of 62, spoke about the huge role that her team had in helping her reach her dream.[78] She spoke about the three things that made sure that she never ever gave up on this dream goal of swimming from Cuba to Florida, and that eventually helped her accomplish it. The first was putting action behind her words and always behaving in a manner that showed that she hadn't given up. The second was believing that dreams have no age limit. And the third was surrounding yourself with the dream team.

The dream team, or your 'dream tribe', believes and has faith in you. The belief they give you unlocks that passion which makes you believe that you will find a way to live your why and reach your dreams. They will be the first ones to encourage you to get back up when you've been knocked down. They will be the ones to encourage you to persist through challenges with fierce determination. They will unlock your passion in a way that keeps you going on your journey with your full heart. They are the ones that help you pursue your dreams and encourage you to find a way to never ever give up. They are the ones that make your journey towards your dreams and goals less solitary and even more incredible. They help you make that journey towards living a life with passion an epic journey of growth.

It's obvious that your dream team might include a very supportive partner, long-lasting friends, some members of your family, and coaches and mentors you've chosen to work with. Sometimes the dream tribe also includes someone you've only met once – but they remain in your dream team because your interaction with them made a lasting impact on you. Many years ago I was on a flight back home to London from Berlin and I had the middle seat in between two very interesting men. On my left, by the window, sat a young man who had been in the same corporate event I had. He spoke passionately about the new covers he'd designed for tablets and was very eager to show some of his latest designs (this was probably because I had told him that at that time I worked for a company who'd just released their first tablet). On my right was another young gentleman who was very eager to talk about my love for riding horses once I let that slip (which isn't hard to happen!).

He started interrogating me (in a way that I actually enjoyed) about what competitive level I was at, which country I rode for at international shows, and what my ambitions were. This simple conversation sparked something in me, and somehow, over the course of this short one and a half hour flight, we came to the conclusion that I was a future Olympian. He proceeded to introduce me to his brother and his friends who sat around us, and he kept using "future Olympian" to introduce me. At the time it made me giggle but very soon afterwards I realised the profound impact his actions had had on me.

I allowed myself to believe that this was feasible. I allowed myself to embrace this ambition. Within weeks of this chance encounter, I started taking steps that would help me train in a more focused way. And since then, I've never let go of this belief. Since then, I've set goals in my riding that work towards this long-term ambition. And if I'm ever in doubt, I simply remember this mystery man on a random flight who rekindled my fire for riding. I remind myself of the feeling that I had when he kept referring to me as "future Olympian". And that's the feeling I carry with me every time I get on the horse. In a very unique way, he is a part of the tribe which keeps my passion alive for my ambitious goals.

In the words of Arianna Huffington, other times your dream tribe might even include a hero or heroine 'in disguise' who inspires you unexpectedly.[79] This could even be a pet or other animal! As a horse rider, you might have probably guessed that my horses have definitely been in my dream tribe in different ways. My first horse gave me the confidence to take up a challenge and start competing. My second horse, Ollie, whom I've owned for 15 years already, has always been my steady rock during rocky times and pushed me to overcome many fears and boundaries. He inspired me to go for my dreams and we both pushed each other to become the best we could be. My third and current competition horse, Mickey, has taught me the real definition of resilience as he's tested my every physical and psychological limit, and continues to do so even today. And then there was my beautiful family dog Chico who I will forever remember as my biggest inspiration for unconditional love. The saying, *"A dog is the only thing in the world that loves you more than it loves itself"*, couldn't be more true, and this alone gives you a sense of self-belief in a way nothing else really can.

Arianna Huffington also talks about eliminating the toxic people from your life who suck out energy and dampen your passion flame rather than lighting it up. (Ok, you might have gathered from these two mentions already that she is in my tribe as one of my inspirations, especially after reading her brilliant book *Thrive* and meeting her in person![80]) It's important to make an effort to build connections with people who are automatically a part of your life, but if there is no real common ground there is no real reason to try and force these people into your tribe. Sometimes people try to forcefully get into your tribe and challenge your views while they're in, and by this time this becomes dangerous as you've already given them some of your trust. Here it's important to reconnect with your authentic self, your meaningful why and your learning self so you remind yourself what it is that's truly important to you.

Personally I had let a very toxic influencer into my tribe just earlier this year. Because they were helping me with something that was very close to my heart (my horses, that is), I had given them my trust and I started to listen to them too much. That is, until they started to challenge my goals, dreams and what I stood for. I started to feel like the odd one out and I didn't feel like I belonged in their environment anymore. That's when my passion flame started to flicker dangerously. This is when I came across a 'hero in disguise' (and he's a key influencer in my tribe still to this day). As I was talking to him about my tiredness and how I felt I was spreading myself too thinly, he said, *"Anything that is not helping you work towards your goals is a distraction"*. One simple sentence and thirteen simple words. It was like magic.

Something clicked in me that made me realise that this other character who had invaded my tribe was trying to now take my focus away from my goals and shift me in a different direction because that would be more beneficial to them. After that simple sentence I realised this person I'd given my trust to didn't deserve it at all, and that they were a very toxic substance in my tribe (and in my life). As I started refocusing on my real why and reconnected with my dreams, I started to see even more toxic elements which reinforced the reality that they had to be removed from my tribe. And very swiftly they were.

This is why staying connected to your true self is vital even when connecting with your tribe. I know which people in my tribe to use for inspiration for what, and I am consistently aware of my real self even when interacting with my trusted tribe members. There is definitely an element of vulnerability in creating real, meaningful connections with your tribe. I introduced Brené Brown's work on vulnerability and courage in Chapter Three and I think it's fitting to repeat some of it here. Yes, it takes courage to be vulnerable and, yes, toxic people who trick you into letting them into your tribe can end up hurting you. But if you don't let your wall down and connect with your authentic sense of vulnerability, you won't whole-heartedly connect with the tribe who has the power to unlock your passion. Even if a toxic person appears every now and then, you'll have the rest of the people in your tribe to help you get back up if you fall down.

Connecting and Technology
In today's age we communicate through many differ-ent mediums, most of which are online. Email, social media and online chats (e.g., WhatsApp, Viber) have changed how we interact with people. Yes, we still meet people and make phone calls, but not like before. This affects the way we connect with each other and our tribe. You may still be able to find answers to some of your questions and feel good after exchanging a few messages with someone in your tribe, yet you may not be getting the full picture or truly learning about each other. Online interaction is a great way to get mini inspiration bursts and perhaps even find new people to include into your tribe. However, online interaction shouldn't fully replace face-to-face inter-action, as it's especially then that you can truly shift each others' energies and light up that passion flame within.

Sherry Turkle justifies this obsession with online interaction as people's desire to have more control: *"Human relationships are rich, and they're messy, and they're demanding. And we clean them up with technology"*.[81] She argues that the online sphere allows us to pre-edit everything we say and share because it gives us time to respond in a way face-to-face communication doesn't. Yet what this is really doing is that it's preventing us from being our true selves and authentically connecting with each other. It's the real conversations we have with others that teach us to have conversations with ourselves.

Research has suggested that on average you check your smartphone 110 times a day and spend about 23 days a year glued to it.[82] That's a full four years over the course of your life! I'm all up for using online measures to stay connected with family and friends abroad (having lived in seven countries I know it helps!), but I also understand that it shouldn't replace face-to-face interaction. What we see in the online sphere can be misleading and remove us from reality, and in fact makes us feel more lost and alone rather than as if we belong.[83]

Connection through technology also brings the danger of social comparison. People use social media in different ways and choose to communicate different things through it, yet people mistakenly assume what they see there is the whole story. Some people use social media to inspire, encourage and celebrate good news in the hopes of inspiring positivity around them. Yet some people take this as the message that their lives are perfect 24/7 and that they never have any misfortunes or challenges. This is when social comparisons become dangerous as people have an unrealistic view of other people's reality and they feel miserable because they feel their reality is somehow worse.[84]

Constantly comparing yourself to others is a quick route to misery if it's not approached in the right way. It's great to have people in your tribe who you look up to and who inspire you, but it's important to approach the view you have of them in the right way so that it's uplifting and energising rather than downputting and deflating. As we explored in the chapter before, adopting a growth mindset is a great first step in helping you use other people's successes as inspiration rather than as a threat. You understand that they are different from you and hence their successes are different too, yet that doesn't make your current successes any smaller. You realise that you can also grow and develop yourself to create similar successes to theirs if that is what you want, and the first step in doing that is openly talking to the people whose successes you admire.

Funnily enough research has also suggested that happy people are less likely to be affected by social comparison.[85] This means that happier people are more likely to notice other people's successes in a more positive way and use them as inspiration. Here you might notice the relevance of the self-reinforcing spiral again. The more you stay true to your authentic self, are open about your why, commit to learning (also from others' successes), and embrace your tribe, the more passionate you will be. The more you unlock your passion, the happier you'll be, and the healthier connections you'll be able to build with your tribe.

It's great to use social media and different online networks to find new like-minded people to introduce into your tribe, but make sure you don't use them to compare yourself against others. Evolve those relationships into face-to-face interactions if you can. In order to really connect with each other, you need the eye contact, the real smiles, the touch and even simply the energy of the person sitting next to you. You need to embrace your vulnerabilities and the vulnerabilities of the people in your tribe because it's through these wholehearted moments that you can truly connect. It's through these connections that you really light up that fire from within.

Connect through Passion

Connecting with others can be a really powerful, uplifting way to unlock your passion. It is very likely that you have already experienced this sensation before, but perhaps have not thought about it in more detail. Becoming more aware of it and making a conscious effort to surround yourself with the people who lift you higher will enable you to fully embrace your passion while helping others unlock theirs. The exercises below will help you to explore your emotional connection to your tribe, how you are already connected with the people in it, and how you can further improve your connection with them.

1. What happens when I connect with like-minded people?

Understanding what you yourself feel when you connect with like-minded people will enable you to see how your tribe helps you light up your inner passion. Awareness of your connections, just like the awareness of the other passion elements, is the first step to embracing them in the most powerful way.

EXERCISE:

How do you feel when you are surrounded by like-minded people?

Sometimes it is simply the energy of the people you are with that influences how you feel. As I mentioned earlier, moods and emotions are incredibly contagious, even more so from people in your tribe who you respect. Think about the effect that the people in your tribe have on you even if you're simply in their company. Your passion is sparked in different ways in different situations but they might all be equally relevant for you. From being in the same room with a supportive partner to going for coffee in a café full of aspiring entrepreneurs to watching a TED talk by someone who inspires you – these can all affect the unlocking of your passion.

Think about the thoughts and feelings that go through your head when you are surrounded by like-minded people. Identify one or two specific experiences that you remember really energised you and lit you up. How did it make you feel? I'll give you two examples of mine to help get your creativity juices flowing.

One of my most uplifting, energising evenings this year was an Alumni event at my university that brought together graduates of the university's positive psychology programme from the last eight years. The evening started with a seminar from a guest speaker which was followed by audience Q&A. The evening wrapped up with networking drinks. The energy in the room in that evening was absolutely incredible. I felt as if I was surrounded by about a hundred amazing souls who were all using positive psychology in their own ways to make their positive mark in the world. I totally felt this buzzing vitality and childlike awe which my interview participants described when I asked them about passion. I felt so alive and so ready to take on the world. My passion was on a real high!

Another example is the horse environment I'm exposed to almost daily. A few years ago I made the decision to move my horse to my trainer's so I could focus on progressing my riding more quickly while still continuing to build my career. Immediately I was sucked into the aspirational energy that my trainer's yard had. Everyone there is very ambitious in their riding goals and focused on achieving them. We are all eager to keep on learning and progressing, and we all support each other in our riding adventures. I feel so much a part of a team and I feel like I really belong there. I get energised and motivated by following the other trainees' journeys, and they feel the same following mine. The minute I step out of my car onto the yard I know it's time to play. Simply the energy of the place gets me even more excited to get on the horse.

EXERCISE:
How do you feel when you are interacting with like-minded people?

The next level of passion unlocking comes from interacting with your tribe. This interaction starts with all kinds of conversations, from sharing stories to discussing best practices to even challenging each other's approaches (as long as their best interest is always kept in mind). Another level of interaction could be working with like-minded people one-to-one or in group situations, for example with colleagues who have similar stories or whys behind the work they do. This could even include random events where you seem to come across people who are like-minded and you instantly connect with them in some way. Think about at least two specific times when you have interacted with like-minded people and how it made you feel.

I have a unique example to share here. My partner organises this fun, friendly dinner get-together a few times every month. It's his way of connecting with old friends while making new friends over good food and good conversation. The only rule for 'The Dinner' is that when you've already been once, the following times you come you have to bring at least one new guest. I've been to a few of them now, and I think it was at my fourth one that I had a moment that time stood still for a reason. I realised I was exactly where I wanted to be, where I needed to be, where I was meant to be. I was interacting with passionate, ambitious young professionals who were all eager to learn more about each other and were open minded to each others' careers, backgrounds and stories. It felt like a safe environment to completely be yourself and every conversation with the different people around the table got my passion flame burning strongly. I felt so at home there while becoming excited and lit up by the whole evening.

I also feel my most passionate when I'm doing coaching sessions, training workshops or keynote talks to my ideal clients. I didn't realise how much the work I do really unlocked my passion until I ran a team-building strengths workshop for a company on their annual away day. It was one of the first training sessions I was running for a big corporate and I was intrigued how it would be received. Little did I know that I'd be walking out of there feeling more passionate than ever. The room was full of different types of people, with some sceptical about the ideas and exercises I was taking them through and others more open. Yet the common denominator was their eagerness to learn and try these new approaches. As I explained the ideas, answered their questions, and helped them work through the exercises, I felt so alive. I felt like I belonged. I felt I was living my why while being my wholehearted self. I felt as if I had just discovered the secret to fulfilment. I felt I was my authentic, passionate self.

2. How am I connecting with my tribe right now?

The previous exercises helped you become more aware of how you feel when you are around like-minded people or interacting with them. This leads us on to exploring how you currently spend your time connecting with your tribe. The next exercises will help you reflect on how varied your interactions are with your tribe and whether you're making the most of your time with them.

> **EXERCISE:**
> When, where and how are you connecting with like-minded people right now?

It's useful to explore the circumstances in which you are most likely to interact with your tribe because it gives you a chance to evaluate them. Think about the different timings, locations and situations when you are connecting with your people. List as many different things as you can, because a bigger list will help you with the next question. Have at least 15 different situations on the list.

As usual, I'll start with some items from my list in the hope of inspiring you to keep your thinking cap on after the previous exercise.

- In training sessions I run in organisations full of ambitious, driven and talented people who are hungry to learn and test new things to become their best possible selves.

- During coaching sessions with my clients. (I often attract my ideal client so they are very similar in their values and eager to learn so they definitely belong in my tribe in a particular way.)
- At conferences that bring together people who are eager to create positive change in their own ways. (The ones who focus on happiness at work, positive psychology, meaning, self-development or innovation seem to attract me the most.)
- At dinners with my friends when we talk about anything from passion to love to life and more.
- At my university's alumni events where people hungry for learning and appreciative of their time at university get together to share their stories and connect.
- At my trainer's stables where I'm surrounded by people with the same love for horses and similar ambitions in their riding.
- At national or international equestrian competitions where the love for horses and the desire to succeed connects everyone together.
- On Facetime, Skype or the phone when I talk to some of the people I love the most in this world. (I have to thank the internet here as I have a lot of loved ones abroad so being able to talk to them 'virtually face-to-face' is a real blessing.) These people are my biggest fans and always help keep my passion going strong.

EXTRA EXERCISE:
Draw your tribe.

This might also be a useful exercise to try to do visually. Draw a circle in the middle that represents you. Then draw another circle that represents your inner tribe – these could be the people who you find you connect with the most. Then draw a third circle that represents your outer tribe – the people and environments that unlock your passion in one way or another, but not to the same extent as the personal connections in your inner tribe do. I've drawn an example of my circle below to give you a flavour of this.

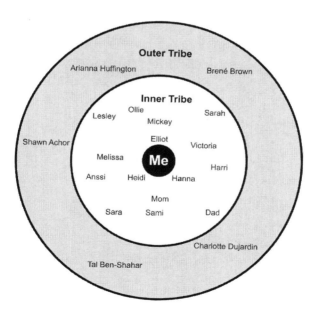

EXERCISE:
Which way of connecting with your tribe do you find most energising and uplifting?

This is an opportunity to explore the list that you already wrote down and think about which ways of connection you find most energising and uplifting. Think about the list you have written down – are the situations on the list mostly at work, in social situations or in other activities? Which of the activities do you find contribute to your life changing for the better in one way or another? Think about the common denominator you see between the things that are on your list.

For example, if you look at my list, you can see most of the activities have something to do with connecting people face-to-face. This shows how I find the sense of belonging that unlocks my passion mainly in offline situations. I crave the full human experience with the smiles, the hugs and the vibe from the other people in order to fully embrace them. You can also see from my list that I feel most passionate when I'm living my why while working with people who appreciate the work I do, as well as when I'm surrounded by people who do similar types of work to me or are interested in it. Another thing that is clear from my list is the mix of places I get my passion unlocked – from training sessions to Skype coaching to social dinners to sporting events. Variety is something that keeps my flame high and that's for a good reason – in fact we are going to discuss variety in depth in the next chapter.

Some of the things in my list have to do with the energy I gain from simply being in a specific type of environment. Since I changed careers and became Happyologist, I have found myself on a self-discovery path of my own which has made me more sensitive to the moods and energies of the people around me. It has also made me more aware of the type of vibe exuded by the environment I'm in, and how this also has a strong influence on unlocking my passion. Because of this, I actively now seek to visit places or areas where the vibe is similar to mine – ambitious, positive and passionate.

3. What can I do to connect more with like-minded individuals?

Having explored how the connections with your tribe make you feel and which of them have the best effect on you, it's now time to explore how to maximise the best opportunities. Motivational speaker Jim Rohn famously said, "*You are the average of the five people you spend the most time with*". This is an opportunity for you to think about if the (five) people you're spending the most time with right now are inspiring and energising you to be your most passionate self.

> **EXERCISE:**
> Come up with at least 10 new opportunities to connect with your people.

Use your answers from the previous exercise to think about the kind of situations and activities that you find most energising and uplifting. How can you create more situations like this? Where could you hang out more to find more like-minded people? What kind of networks could you join to find your passion crew? Think creatively here (use the Cheat Sheet if you need to), identifying some opportunities that might be similar to your existing activities and also completely new, non-ordinary ones that might be a bit of risk but could pay out in the end.

I can think of a few opportunities for me already. From my previous response you probably noticed I like to connect face-to-face, yet there are a multitude of communities online that I could explore in more depth. In the hopes of inspiring you, here are some opportunities, some usual and some unusual for me, that I am going to commit to:

- Join an online network of authors in the self-help, non-fiction and psychology genres. Together we can explore each others' learnings, challenges and successes to unlock each others' passion.
- Become more active in LinkedIn groups that focus on practising positive psychology in organisations. This is an opportunity to network and connect with people who are likely to have similar whys to mine.
- Find self-development meet ups that revolve around helping people become their best

possible selves. As someone who's always looking to learn and improve, as well as help others to learn and improve, this could be a new way to connect with people with similar interests.

- Attend a unique conference, event or educational festival that attracts people who want to live their best possible lives. I have a few on my list that I've wanted to go to for a while but never have – now is the time!
- Find out the most popular London cafés for entrepreneurs to work from and embrace the energy of their passionate souls.

It's time for you to think out of the box now. List at least 10 specific opportunities and use the Cheat Sheet questions at the end of this book to help you come up with new ideas if you get stuck.

EXERCISE:
What can you do daily to connect with like-minded people to keep your energy high?

Last but not least it's time to identify how you can connect with your tribe daily to keep that passion flame burning strong. It's easier to keep it alive than to constantly let it die down and then set it alight all over again. That doesn't mean that you don't have downtime or alone time for self-reflection because both of those are critical in helping you connect with your authentic self. However, it does mean that you make an active effort to have some kind of daily inspiration or human connection to keep the flame alive.

Explore a few different options here as some days you might opt for a quick fix and other days you might desire something more powerful. It's ok to think about how you already connect with your like-minded people daily if you do that, but perhaps then look at new ways of doing it as well. For example, as I love my human connections I like to speak to someone in my tribe daily – be it over Facetime, Skype, phone, email or social media if not face-to-face. Even simple interactions such as a five-minute call can get my passion all fired up. However, I would like to make more of an effort to also meet someone from my tribe face-to-face daily.

I often do meet someone from my tribe when I go and train with my horse (which happens four to six times a week depending on the week and my work commitments), but I'd like these interactions to be more around my values, my why or my motivation to master my learning self. This could be anything from a cup of coffee with a friend to a dinner with my partner to a meeting with a client to hanging out in an environment that energises me. I also want to make more of an effort to connect with like-minded people on social media more actively. I feel as if I do spend some time on social media (a bit too much sometimes) but I'd like my time there to be more targeted to interacting with people or groups who are more like-minded to my values and my why.

Find Your People

Connecting with the different people in your tribe not only unlocks your passion but also connects you with your authentic self. Interacting with them in unique ways teaches you things about yourself you wouldn't otherwise learn. Here is a reminder of how connecting with your tribe helps you live a more passionate life:

1. You don't have to do it on your own. In fact, the more you surround yourself with inspirational, energising people who encourage you to live your most passionate life, the better.

2. The connections you make and the relationships you build are one of the most influential aspects of your life, not only in helping you unlock your passion but also in helping you live your most fulfilling life (and yes, these two are connected). Make sure to make time to connect with your tribe in different ways.

3. Go out of your comfort zone when it comes to connecting with your tribe. This is often when it becomes most rewarding as you discover a completely new type of 'out-of-the-box' thinking with someone you didn't realise could be a part of your tribe. Explore new opportunities both online and offline when it comes to connecting with the people who energise your positive passion energy.

With them you find a sense of belonging as you feel understood and appreciated for who you are. They fuel your confidence to be your dynamic authentic self and to live your why, while supporting you in your growth journey towards your dreams. They don't take away your responsibility to proactively choose to be your most passionate self, rather they hold you accountable for that choice while energising you to choose it.

Set your life on fire. Seek those who fan your flames.
~ Rumi ~

seven

Play with Your Strengths

Success is achieved by developing your strengths,
not by eliminating your weaknesses.
~ Marilyn vos Savant ~

The fifth and final element that has the power to unlock your passion is putting your strengths to good use in different ways. Your strengths refer to your natural abilities and skills that are either innate or have been nurtured throughout your life. They are the things you often find easy because they come to you so instinctively. They are the things people regularly praise you for as they notice you using them because of the ease with which you do them and because of the way your passion shines through when you're using them.

These strengths can be interpreted and approached from many different angles. The different psychometric strengths tools out there have shown how this is the case (and I'll discuss them in turn later in this chapter). Some refer to a strength as an underlying psychological characteristic that is desirable to hold, others refer to it as a 'business skill' you're naturally good at. However, the consensus about strengths is that they are not technical skills that you have developed and mastered over time. Neither are they learned behaviours. They are the traits you are naturally strong in. It's possible and likely that these traits have played a part in helping you develop your technical skills, but your strong technical skills shouldn't be seen as your natural strengths. For example, see being analytical as a strength if you excel in creating advanced logarithms on Excel to analyse different business scenarios. See communication and connecting with people as your strength if you are an excellent negotiator or sales person.

Also think about going past the traditional work ideas of what strengths are, and see appreciation, optimism, love and generosity as strengths. These are the more value-driven 'human' strengths which have the power to make a difference in the here and now. These are the strengths that connect you with your authentic self and your why in a more meaningful way. These are the kind of strengths that unlock your passion with fierce intensity.

Using your innate value-driven strengths unlocks your passion in two steps. First, it encourages you to acknowledge that you have natural strengths and also to believe in the positive impact their use can create. Secondly, acknowledging your strengths gives you the confidence to use them in different ways rather than tying them to one specific activity or medium.

The common saying, "*Variety is the spice of life*", is applicable here in that, "*A varied use of your strengths is the spice of passion*". It's specifically the choice to use your strengths in diverse ways that adds to that passion spice within you. It's the novelty factor of using your strengths in different ways that keeps the fire inside of you alive.

This passion flame that is enhanced by the use of your strengths is also fed by the positive emotions and improved performance you experience when you use your strengths. In fact, strengths fuelling your happiness, performance and passion are all interlinked. The different 'side effects' of using your strengths reinforce your passion alongside your authenticity, your why and your learning self, while also connecting you with the people in your tribe who appreciate watching you use your strengths. This is an opportunity for you to make the most of the things you're naturally good at and use them to get in touch with your most passionate self. This is your chance to get creative with the skills you've been given and put them to good use so you can fully live your why.

Passion and Strengths
The relationship between using your strengths and being your most passionate self is tighter than you think. Many decades of research on strengths has already highlighted how using them has numerous benefits to you, your well-being and your performance.[86] Now I am also introducing the tie between strengths and being passionate.

The people I interviewed in my research spoke about how they felt their passion rise when they were using their strengths with great pride and self-belief. Some of the things they said were:

- *"I want to use the skills that I have".*
- *"There's a lot of discovery in finding out what you can do, what other people will join in with and let you do, and then a further discovery of is there a way to incorporate that into working".*
- *"If you're not in alignment with what you're here to do or how the skills you've been given can be put to best use, you're going to experience conflict".*

It was clear these passionate people had the desire to use their natural strengths because they believed in them. They knew that they had traits and qualities that were completely natural to them, and they understood how discovering them and using them brought out their passion. The third quote above also highlights the discomfort they felt when they weren't able to use their strengths. They felt distressed and struggled to perform. The forceful use of their weaknesses and the lack of being able to do what they did best extinguished their passion and exhausted their wellbeing. This clearly showed how being able to do what you do best is a key ingredient in unlocking your passion.

Existing research in strengths has already high-lighted numerous benefits of using your strengths. Endorsing them in the workplace, be it simply knowing them, understanding them and/or using them, has been connected to wellbeing, meaning and job satisfaction.[87] Being able to use them at work has been identified as one of the key drivers of employee engagement,[88] which further supports the idea that when you are able to do something you're naturally good at you don't only enjoy it more but you also perform better.[89]

The benefits of using your strengths at work are also felt beyond the workplace. When you're able to use your natural skills you find yourself feeling more energised and well-rested, both of which further fuel motivation.[90] Here you can see the links to the buzzing vitality and childlike energy passionate people speak of. This shows how using your strengths has the power to connect you to that passion energy. Beyond that, being aware of your strengths, understanding them, and using them also promotes a sense of authenticity and self-determination, which not only improves motivation and performance but further connects you to your passion.[91] This brings us back to Ryan and Deci's self-determination model, which indicates competency drives motivation, with competency here referring to being able to use one's strengths.[92] In a way you can see a whole passion spiral of positive energy, drive and determination light up when you learn to use your strengths in different ways.

Another study found that educating people to use their strengths led to higher levels of engagement, positive emotion, sense of achievement, positive self-concept and attention to the positive.[93] As discussed earlier in the book, positive emotions can further unlock your passion by enabling you to more efficiently activate and access the learning centres in your brain, and hence fully embrace your learning self. Being aware of your strengths makes you feel good about yourself and hence you're more likely to achieve things and work towards fulfilling your full potential.[94] You find an authentic source of energy from your best natural qualities when you build this kind of purposeful, personal connection with them.

This personal connection also has a lot to do with believing in your best traits and what you can do with them. It is this confidence in them that makes it possible for you to use them in different ways while you follow your why to create the positive impact you're looking to create. Acknowledging, understanding and believing in your strengths means that you can find a way to create positive impact in something that you're naturally good at. People who use their strengths to achieve their goals are more likely to achieve them while feeling more fulfilled and happy with reaching them.[95] This suggests that if you identify living your why as your daily and long-term goal, using your strengths while living your why will make it more likely for you to succeed.

It is also the varied use of your strengths that enhances the likelihood of success, be it in better unlocking your passion, experiencing more positive emotions, and/or performing better. This is similar to the idea of having one overarching, prominent why in your life yet potentially still having smaller, more specific whys in your different life domains. Equally, being aware of your main strengths and being able to use them is the key to connecting with them, yet it is by using them in different ways that your passion is most readily unlocked. The most effective way to look at this is to see how you can use your strengths in the best possible way to live your why, and use this as your prominent motivator. The next step is to identify how you can still put your strengths to use in a variety of ways, keeping in mind both day-to-day activities and long-term pursuits.

For example, one of the people I interviewed had a great love for music and for using it to bring people together. You could say her strengths were appreciation of beauty (in the music), love (bringing people together), and communication (connecting with people). She spoke about how she engaged in different activities for different purposes and to have a more passionate balance across her life. She used singing as a tool to help people and in order to bring them together, yet she used dance to relax and escape from her usual world. She was still using her strengths in these different instances but in very different ways and with a different purpose behind them.

Someone else I interviewed described how they used their strengths of communication and connection to work with groups of people, but with different groups of people in different circumstances in different ways. This type of variety keeps things dynamic and constantly evolving, connecting you with your learning self. In a way, it's about always creating and uncovering new ways of putting your strengths to good use. This again is aligned with existing research on strengths that highlights how using them in different ways makes you happier and more fulfilled and helps you perform better.[96]

It's this variety of use that also helps to ensure that you are not overusing your strengths. Just as you need balance in order to keep control of your passion when it's unlocked, you need to do the same with your strengths. If you become too reliant on them, they can become more unhelpful than helpful and actually prevent you from succeeding.[97] For example, my strength of persistence can lead to obsessive, inflexible tenacity and stubbornness if overused. I always make sure I am using this strength in different areas of my life and in different ways because it helps me to stop, reflect and re-evaluate if I'm persisting with the right things (and helps me to know when not to persist). Using your strengths in different ways creates a more all-round experience which makes you more self-aware of how you are using them and keeps you in the driving seat.

Strengths are the last missing piece in unlocking your passion yet you can see that piece is closely linked to the other four pieces. The more aware you are of your strengths, the more connected you will be with your authentic self (and vice versa). The more you are able to use your strengths in different ways, the more you'll continue learning and growing. The more you have confidence in your strengths, the easier it will be to stay focused on and persist with living out your why. Last but not least, the more you use your strengths with different people, the more authentic, meaningful connections you will build with your tribe.

Discovering Your Strengths
To a certain extent you are free to discover your strengths through simple reflection, and by becoming more aware

of what you find easy and enjoyable. Some of the exercises at the end of this chapter will help you think about exactly that. On the other hand, there are several tools you can use if you want some inspiration and perhaps some sort of objective validity to your strengths ownership. These tools are psychometrically validated tests that enable you to identify your strengths through a series of questions you answer.

However, before I dive into the tools themselves, let's explore the first way of discovering your strengths: through self-reflection. In order to do this, it's important to understand what using your strengths actually feels like. Martin Seligman describes the experience of using your strengths in the following way:[98]

- You feel connected to your authentic self.
- You feel excited and energised.
- You are eager to learn even more about using them.
- You like to use them in new ways with existing skills.
- You yearn to use them.
- You feel unable to stop yourself from using them.
- You find yourself getting involved in activities and projects which bring them out of you.
- You feel enthusiastic and joyful.

If these points fail to give you clarity on your strengths, the second strategy is to use a variety of psychometrically validated tools to explore yourself. The Values in Action Strengths (referred to as VIA Strengths) is my personal favourite tool because in a way it presents strengths as human qualities that could equally be seen as someone's values. This tool defines strengths as an underlying psychological characteristic that is valued in its own right, desired as a quality just as it is.[99] It's no surprise that this particular tool was developed by Martin Seligman, who was one of the founding fathers of positive psychology, and the late Christopher Peterson. The 24 strengths they identify fall into six categories referred to as human virtues: wisdom and knowledge; courage; love and humanity; justice; temperance; and spirituality and transcendence.[100] Some examples of their strengths include hope, optimism, gratitude and appreciation of beauty and excellence. You can take a free version of the survey online at VIA Strengths and receive a short description of your top five strengths, also defined as your signature strengths.

Another positive psychology driven strengths tool is the Realise2 developed by the Centre for Applied Positive Psychology (CAPP).[101] Their model goes a step further than the VIA Strengths by separating strengths into realised and unrealised strengths, identifying weaknesses, and suggesting learned behaviours. Some examples of their 60 strengths include detail, connector, listener, improver and resolver. The tool's aim is to help you distinguish your strengths from your learned behaviours, as well as potentially develop weaknesses into learned behaviours if they need to be learned. The model aims to offer a more holistic view of an individual as it doesn't ignore your weaknesses yet still focuses on you making the most of your strengths. Identifying your weaknesses can help you reflect on whether you are unconsciously having to use them in your life or career at the moment, and can prompt you to take action if this is the case. These are the traits that drain your energy and can block your passion so being aware of them is of benefit.

Gallup, an organisation that has been researching human behaviour since the middle of the twentieth century, also has a strengths tool of its own. StrengthsFinder 2.0, written by Tom Rath, identifies strengths that are more business focused.[102] Some examples of their 34 strengths include analytical, consistency, focus, relator and strategic. The tool itself is based on a 40-year study of human strengths so there is plenty of validity behind it. Yet I still stand by my reflection that most of the strengths they identify are more relevant for the workplace rather than life overall. Saying that, if you want to explore these tools in more detail, I recommend playing with each of them to get a fully holistic view. There's no harm in testing them all out, as long as you don't overwhelm yourself with the different approaches you experience and perhaps varied responses you see. Simply take what you connect with the most with your intuition, and remember to reflect on your strengths as well (and you'll get a chance to do that later in this chapter!).

As these tools are self-rated they are a subjective perception of yourself and your abilities. However, as they have all been tested for their reliability and validity it's more likely than not that they will highlight many truths.

The third (what I like to call) fun way to explore your strengths is to ask the people who you've interacted with what they think your strengths are. These people don't necessarily have to be in the tribe that I spoke about in the previous chapter. Sometimes even someone you've met once or twice can have some interesting insights because your strengths often shine through quite clearly when you are meeting people for the first time.

This activity balances out the intrinsic view you get from reflecting on your strengths and from working with a strengths tool. This activity shows an extrinsic perspective on your strengths as you're giving the people who know you the chance to tell you what strengths they associate you with. Here are the simple steps to get this fun strengths activity under way.

1. Set up a free survey online (such as a Google form or Survey Monkey) that has one simple question: "*What are my top three qualities?*" Have three text spaces underneath so that the people can write one quality in each box. Set-up the survey in a way that people respond anonymously and let them know that this is the case. This will make them feel more comfortable in being completely honest.

2. Send the link to the survey to 30 people you know from across your lifetime and from different areas of your life. For example, send it

to some your current close friends and some of your friends from when you were growing up. Send it to different family members. Send it to your old high school teachers and some of the professors that knew you better in university. Send it to your old colleagues and bosses if you can, as well as some of the current ones you can trust. (If you're feeling self-conscious about sending this out and worried about what people will think, just call it a self-development project you're working on – or whatever you feel comfortable with. People will be very intrigued by it and happy to help!)

3. Give them a deadline to complete the survey (a few weeks or so) and wait for the responses to flow in.

4. Enjoy the feelings of pride, appreciation and joy as you see the responses that praise you come in. It's incredibly uplifting and humbling!

5. Create a final list of top five strengths after you've seen most of the responses come in. See the similarities in people's responses and see which qualities seem to appear repeatedly.

6. Now think about how this list compares to the strengths you identified yourself through self-reflection and through the psychometric strengths tools if you used them.

This is a very powerful exercise that not only starts connecting you with your authentic self through awareness of your strengths, but it also improves your self-esteem. It basically shows you the strengths you're portraying to the outside world as people report what they think you portray in the most passionate way. The bonus of this exercise is that it gives you a great feel-good vibe as well. Embrace the responses you get and be proud of them. Let each of them give you more confidence, passion and positivity. Let each of them help you stand taller and motivate you to use them in new ways.

Using a combination of self-reflection, self-rated strengths tools and feedback from others on your strengths is a secure way forward. Together they will give you a holistic perspective on your strengths, and show your potential in the varied responses you get. Stay open minded to what you see, and don't take it as the final be all and end all. Some situations might bring out different strengths in you, and you may enjoy using different strengths throughout the different phases in your life. The key, as with the other passion elements, is to stay in touch with your authentic dynamic self. Continuously check back on which of the strengths are giving you most enjoyment, helping you perform at your best, and unlocking your positive passion energy.

Play with Your Natural Abilities

Strengths are the fifth and final element in connecting you with your most passionate self. Acknowledging that you have natural positive abilities, becoming more aware of them, and learning to use them in different ways with confidence will turn your passion into its most powerful form. The exercises below will help you think about what your strengths are, how using them makes you feel, how you are already using them, and how you could use them in new ways.

1. What are my top five strengths?

I encourage you to explore your strengths with some of the tools I shared, but I urge you to start with the self-reflection questions here before taking the tools. The tools are incredibly useful in getting you to identify your strengths but if you use them before actually thinking about your strengths they can give you a bias which might influence how you perceive your strengths. Because of this, I encourage you to connect with your authentic strengths right here right now before putting them to the test on a tool.

EXERCISE:

What are your top five strengths in life? Try to identify the five things that come most naturally to you.

This is the first step to starting to identify your strengths through self-reflection. This is your opportunity to think about your best qualities and traits. Think about the things that come really naturally to you, and the traits people often say they admire in you. These are the things you often find so easy and instinctive that when others praise you for them you're often left surprised because you're thinking, "Well isn't everyone like this?" Try to avoid looking at superficial technical skills which represent proficiency, knowledge or aptitude in a specific occupation, field or industry. Go deeper than that and explore the positive qualities and traits you feel have been dominant throughout your life. It could be that these traits and qualities have played a role in shaping and improving your technical skills, and play a role in your day-to-day life and career even when your technical skills are not in action.

There is no real rule or limitation to what you identify as your strength as long as it's not a learned skill. For example, you could be very skilled at using Excel to create mathematical models that predict the rising value of a specific property. That in itself isn't a strength but the strengths that could have enabled you to find that particular skill easy could include being analytical and appreciating beauty and excellence (i.e. attention to detail). The strengths I'm encouraging you to identify could be anything from being naturally analytical or strategic to being instinctively kind or optimistic or grateful. Think about more 'human' traits that could come out in all kinds of situations, not purely at work.

Something that will help you identify some of your strengths is thinking about a time when you were performing at your best. When was the last time you were working on something that was really important to you and you felt that your best qualities were coming out because you were having fun while excelling in your performance? Thinking back to an experience like this, be it back in your studies, in your current workplace, at home, or in a social situation, can help you identify the qualities that made success happen in that instant.

My example of this is giving my first talk at a TEDx conference in London.[103] I have always been a strong communicator and confident presenter, yet it was that moment and milestone that shone light on many of my key strengths. As I do keynote talks regularly to large audiences and run training workshops to sometimes sceptical groups of people, I had no problem stepping on stage. Yet I felt there was this added pressure that came from the talk sitting under the TEDx brand. I prepared for days for that talk on passion and my nerves were still jiggling when they were hooking the microphone onto my back before I went on stage. And when I stepped on stage, the nerves disappeared. The words came out confidently from my mouth and the engaged audience was right with me every step of the way. The energy in the room was palpable, and I was almost in awe of the undivided attention every member of the audience gave me. I felt I was performing at my best, and I felt that the audience was helping me do that.

That moment reminded me of my top five strengths. The first of those was definitely persistence. The road to having got to speak at TEDx wasn't an overnight one but my focus and persistence led me to being on stage at that moment. My persistence in working on my talk and my slides made it flow exactly how I wanted it to. This goes in hand with one of my other strengths: appreciation for beauty and excellence. I made sure that the talk ticked the boxes for what makes a talk excel, and I made sure every detail on my slides made them aesthetically pleasing. My strength of being a natural learner also played a huge role in being on that stage. I had learned about best practices of TED talks to fine tune my talk, and of course my strength of learning led me to do the research that revealed this new approach to passion that was the subject of my talk (the approach you're reading about now). It was also my strength of gratitude which shone through as I felt so appreciative of being able to be on that stage, from having the support of friends and family in my journey to get there to having the attention of the 100-strong audience in the room. Last but not least, my strength of connecting with people shone through. I've always been very empathetic and understanding, and I use those traits to tell stories on stage that help people connect with me. On that stage in that moment, I felt I was living and breathing my strengths.

EXERCISE:
How do you feel when you use your strengths?

I already explained how a key hint that one of your positive qualities is a strength is when you actually enjoy using that trait. You often experience positive emotions, such as joy and pride, when you know you are using your strengths and also when you are being praised for them. So now that you have identified your top five strengths through self-reflection, it's time to think about how you actually feel when you use them. (If you haven't been able to identify your top five strengths or don't feel too confident about your choices, have a play with the strengths tools now if you feel stuck.) What are the thoughts going through your head when you know you are using your strengths? How do you feel when you are using them? How do you feel when they help you perform at your best? You can think about these questions overall, or even use the example of you performing at your best from the previous question to think about how you felt when you were doing that.

When I am using my learning strength I feel that I am getting closer to fulfilling my potential. I feel excited to be exploring something new, as if I'm on an adventure of self-development. I feel most connected to my authentic self and proud of being who I am. I feel confident I can learn to deal with any new situation or overcome any challenge, and proud that I'm not afraid to ask for help from more experienced people so that I can learn from the best. When I use my strength of gratitude, I feel that I am connecting with humankind. I believe the whole world could use a little more appreciation and I feel blessed to have it come so naturally to me. I feel more connected to my heart and my being when I let it come out. When I am connecting with people I feel at my happiest. I was not surprised at all when I discovered the research that shows a huge part of human happiness has to do with having positive relationships with people. I totally get that, and again I feel grateful that I find that easy and very fulfilling. Overall, using my strengths makes me feel that I am connected to my authentic self and that I am doing my best to create as much positive impact as possible in the world. And best of all, it really makes me feel alive. It really lights up that fire inside of me that drives me to keep going forward in my life of adventure.

2. What is my current connection with my strengths?

Now that you have become more aware of what your strengths are, the next step is to become aware of how you are already using them. This gives you the opportunity to maximise the current use of your strengths to their full potential. It also helps you to evaluate whether you enjoy how you are using them now or whether there is something you would like to change.

EXERCISE:
How are you using your strengths at the moment?

Think about the five strengths you identified in the earlier question. Ask yourself in which areas of your life they are currently coming through the strongest. Don't limit yourself – let the answers come to you. They could be coming through in your job, at home, with your friends, or maybe in a hobby. How are they coming through in them? Are they coming through in specific situations, such as when you feel you are being challenged, or when you are being asked to show how something is done? Or do you find you are using them regularly throughout your working day? The more detailed your answers, the more self-awareness you will build. It will also make it much easier for you to make the most of the questions that follow on optimising the use of your strengths.

Gratitude is the strength I use in every interaction I have with someone. I always voice my appreciation to a friend for making the time to see me, to a family member for always being supportive and helping me through a challenge, to a client for giving me the opportunity to work with them, to my trainer for helping me progress in my riding, and to my horse for having a positive reaction to something I asked from him. My strength of learning shines through when I'm writing a new blog post or article for a publication. I want to make sure I'm sharing the latest research on the topic so I read up to learn more about the topic or a specific angle of it. I'm also often looking to learn how to be as efficient as possible in some of the mundane activities of life, such as housework or the admin involved in running a business. I seek to connect with people who are in my field to learn from them and I actively attend seminars or events where I can learn from the best in my field. I invest a lot in training with my horse because every day I get on I want to learn something new.

Persistence shines through in many aspects of my life. I persist in following-up on potential client leads and showing them the value I would add to them. I persist through business ups and downs, continuing to believe in myself and my business even when I don't secure a particular client I was really looking forward to working with. I persist in the equestrian sport a little bit like a mad woman (if you're a rider you'll know exactly what I'm talking about!). I have my tumbles, my falls and injuries from riding, and so does the horse. I patiently persist in perfecting my body coordination to better communicate with my horse, and persist at asking for something even when he puts up a fight. I have learned to master the art of flexible persistence especially through riding because every day you sit on your horse you are riding a different beast with different thoughts and different levels of suppleness. You need to be able to adjust your approach very quickly onboard yet also know when to persist with a particular approach. As my trainer says, *"Ride what's underneath you right now."*

My strength of connection is aligned with my gratitude strength as it often helps me connect with people further. I am using it throughout every day – be it from writing a blog post or article that helps me connect with the audiences online to doing one-to-one coaching sessions with individuals to facilitating a training workshop to help you find love in your job.

Last but not least, my strength of appreciating beauty and excellence shines through everything I do. Every blog and article is written, edited, re-read and proofread to make it as 'excellent' as possible for my readers. Every image I use on my blog needs to have aesthetically pleasing elements in it that connect with human emotions. The training programmes and workshops I run are being continuously perfected, and what I present is as important as how I present it (from my appearance to how I design my slides). I appreciate beautifully designed websites, scenery that takes your breath away, and design that is not only beautiful but also practical. This appreciation of beauty and excellence is probably something that led me to the equestrian sport of dressage, which is all about perfecting the harmony between horse and rider while looking absolutely flawless. To me, a world class Grand Prix test performed flawlessly is the definition of beauty and excellence.

EXERCISE:
Which of your five strengths do you enjoy using the most, and in what situations? Which of the strengths unlock your passion energy in the most powerful way?

It may be hard to have favourites among your different strengths and the situations you use them in because they are all probably giving you enjoyment in some form. Explore what kind of enjoyment you find in the strengths. Which ones give you anticipation excitement, joy when you're using them, or fulfilment after you've used them? When do you feel your most positive, energised and free self when using your strengths? When do you feel your most passionate self? Evaluating the current use of your strengths will help you make the most of them.

This question is a challenge for me as well; something that has helped me to work through this is thinking about the strengths I tend to stay more in control of. For example, persistence comes to me very naturally yet sometimes I overuse it in a particular area to the extent that it stops being enjoyable. When I do have it under control, I still feel proud, excited and energised because I am persisting through challenging situations. Hence the enjoyment I gain from using persistence is more achievement driven. On the other hand, learning really pushes the high energy, feel-good buttons for me. It matches with so many of my values and makes me feel I am trying to be the best version of me so that I can discover how to create as much positive impact as possible. When I am reading a book I really connect with, I feel excitement, joy, freedom and awe. When I have a training session with my horse learning a new movement I feel out of this world yet completely one with it. I feel love, hope and appreciation for the sport I do. I feel I am my most passionate when I am learning.

Similarly, taking a moment to be grateful for everything I have daily makes me feel humble, loved and appreciated in return. Saying thanks to people who light up my fire, support me in my adventures and give their perspective on a challenge makes me feel whole. Yet I think gratitude brings a sense of calmness and serenity rather than sparking my passion. I think it's a strength that helps maintain the passion at a healthy level rather than firing it up. Appreciating beauty and excellence on the other hand gets me excited and energised. I feel enthusiastic in my activities when I take a moment to appreciate the beauty and excellence around me. This could be anything from running a workshop at a super inspiring environment to taking a walk down my street to watching my horse move with graceful power in the field. It could be watching a movie that's been beautifully directed, or seeing an inspirational TED talk by someone who's truly an expert in their field. To me, my most passionate self comes out when I am using my strength of connecting in order to connect with my tribe. Be they through the phone or face-to-face, human interactions with my tribe help bring out my passion the most when it comes to my strength of connecting.

3. How can I use my top five strengths in new, unique ways?

Last but not least, it's time to explore how to diversify the use of your strengths. The key to using your strengths to unlock your passion is to use them in a variety of ways. It could be that you are expressing them in different areas of your life, in different forms, or simply in a new shape. But it is this variety that keeps you in control of your passion, and keeps that sense of adventure and excitement alive.

EXERCISE:
Think about three new ways you could use each of your strengths.

As you've already explored how you are using your strengths in different life domains, I encourage you to think about how else you could use them on top of what you do already. Make sure what you put on your list makes you excited to do it. Yes, it can be scary and intimidating and push you out of your comfort zone – but you still need to want to do it. Think about the responses to your previous question on how you are using your strengths when you feel most passionate. Could you transfer your enjoyment of using a particular strength with one activity to another one? Or from one life domain to another? Or even from one specific type of interaction to another? The questions on the Cheat Sheet (on page 233) can really help you through this one.

Here are some new ways I am going to commit to using my favourite strengths to bring out more of my passion. Hopefully they'll inspire you to get started on your list!

> - Learning: I love learning through books, TED talks, training sessions and watching experts in action. Yet I want to try learning something completely new and random to have a bit of an adventure. I want to learn how to make a Victoria Sponge cake and make the jam in it from scratch. I also want to learn speed reading so I can tackle more non-fiction books in an effective way. I want to do an improvisation course just for the fun of it!
> - Appreciation of beauty and excellence: I want to appreciate the beauty of uncertainty in day-to-day

life. From the unpredictable English weather (yes, four seasons in a day is possible here!) to a spontaneous, unplanned Saturday to not knowing how the new dish I'm making will taste. I want to appreciate the beauty of the unknown so I can find the passion in the uncertainty.

- Persistence: I want to use my persistence to keep trying new types of meditation practices. I have tried a few that I haven't liked but I want to persist at finding the right one for me because I know it will improve my self-awareness, focus and wellbeing – all of which will naturally help me to build an even stronger connection with my passion within.

EXERCISE:
How could you remind yourself to use one of your strengths in a different way every day?

Here you can bring in something that you put on your list in the previous question, or think of an even simpler way to use one of your strengths differently today than you used it yesterday. Think about a trigger that would remind you of it daily, regardless of where you are or what you are doing. It could be something you start the day with, reflect on during your lunchtime or spend a moment mid-afternoon to think about whether you have used your strength in a new way today. Sometimes you also use strengths in new ways subconsciously, which means that you are putting them into action but not necessarily noticing them right then and there. This is why reflecting on your day could help make you aware of how you've already used your strength in a new way. Or perhaps you want to set yourself a daily schedule. Mondays, Wednesdays and Fridays you could use five minutes at the start of your day to think about how you are going to implement your strengths in a new way at work. Tuesdays and Thursdays you may want to do something with your strengths outside work. Weekends you could take the more spontaneous route and not plan for it. The more you practise your strengths in different ways, the easier it will become to think of new ways and the more instinctive it will become in your day-to-day life.

When you start to put this into practice, the key is to think about what kind of reminders usually work for you. If you are trying to build a new habit or eliminate an old bad one, what kind of triggers have you used to remind yourself of the new habit or to stop yourself from doing the bad habit? A reminder in your calendar, a charm on your bracelet, a picture on your phone, or a certain ringtone? Think about what would remind you and excite you to use your strengths. For example, I have a lion charm on my bracelet that reminds me to be brave and strong like a lion so I can use my strengths in a new way. I also have an ornament in my bedroom that reminds me of variety, which I interpret as a sign of encouragement to use my strengths in a variety of ways. My daily habit of writing down my achievements for the day and the top priorities for the next day also helps me think about whether I used a strength in a new way, and if not, I write it down as a priority for the next day.

Be Your Best Most Passionate You

This is an opportunity for you to connect with what you do best and use it to unlock your passion in the most powerful way. Remember these three points if nothing else to make the most of your natural abilities:

1.   Start by self-reflection to identify your strengths to avoid tool bias or being boxed in. Explore what your natural abilities are by thinking about what skills you find easy, enjoyable and energising to use.
2.   Contemplate on which of your strengths are coming out in what situations. Identify the strengths you find most energising and uplifting to use, and think about why that is the case. Try to put your favourite strengths to use more often to unlock even more of your passion.
3.   Really push yourself to pursue variety with your strengths. It's using them in new ways or in new situations that makes them the most powerful and impactful.

Treat your life as an adventure and have fun with the different ways you can use your natural strengths. Be brave and adventurous with your best traits, and you'll realise how invigorating and fun it is to play with them in new ways. Again, the choice is yours. Choose to use your best traits to unlock your passion.

If we all did the things we are capable of, we would astound ourselves.
~ Thomas Edison ~

PART III:

SHARING YOUR PASSION

WITH THE WORLD

eight

Spread Passion at Work

One person with passion is better than
forty people merely interested.
~ E. M. Forster ~

Learning to connect with the five passion keys means that you can choose to be passionate throughout your life. This means you don't need to go find your passion in order to find happiness and your best performance at work. You have the opportunity right now to unlock your passion and find love in what you already do at work. You don't need to change roles, departments or careers to get in touch with your passion. All you need to do is to commit to becoming passionate at work.

Earlier on we discussed the numerous benefits of living your whole life with passion. They apply as much to your workplace as they do to your overall life. Imagine feeling more joyful, proud and happy at work. Imagine connecting to your work in a meaningful way that makes you feel more fulfilled. These feelings will further fuel the passion that you bring in as well as spread the passion to the people around you at work.

Passion and Motivation

Motivation has been discussed over decades through various theories and models. Here I am going to briefly introduce to you the most popular model of intrinsic motivation in positive psychology in order to demonstrate how passion goes even beyond the power of motivation. Intrinsic motivation is the drive that exists within yourself that motivates you to do something without relying on a desire for reward or being pushed to act through external pressures. Basically, when you are intrinsically motivated to do something, it's because you find enjoyment, and possibly even fulfilment, through doing it.

As briefly mentioned earlier, Ryan and Deci's theory of self-determination highlights autonomy, competence and relatedness as the drivers of intrinsic motivation.[104] Autonomy is the urge to direct your own life, so that you take control of it and make the choices you want. Competence refers to being able to do whatever's asked of you, which is driven by your belief that you have the skills to do it. Last but not least, relatedness means being able to relate to others through what you're doing. Basically Ryan and Deci said you will feel intrinsically motivated if you feel that you're in control of what you're doing, if you believe you have the skills to do it, and if it helps you connect with other people.

Daniel Pink also introduced his version of intrinsic motivation in his book *Drive* – and his TED talk is also one of the most watched TED talks of all time.[105] He adapted Ryan and Deci's model to the three similar components of autonomy, mastery and purpose. You can see the overlap of being able to be in control of your own life, with the additional elements of the desire to improve in something to the level of being a master at it, and the purposeful yearning to do something in the service of something larger than ourselves.

There are definite links between passion and intrinsic motivation. Intrinsic motivation comes from being able to direct your life, having a sense of purpose, using your skills and connecting with other people. However, to be intrinsically motivated, you have to direct your focus onto something and apply these keys to that particular activity. This can prove to be quite limiting. These five keys to unlocking your passion that I've shared with you help you to inject passion into everything you do, not only to the few things you feel you are able master.

Through unlocking your passion, you learn to be the authentic you throughout your life, to continuously seek ways to create positive impact, to learn and to grow in whatever you're doing, to connect with the people who propel you forward, and to put your natural strengths to use in different ways. It is true that these passion keys will give you motivation and drive – but also so much more. They will help you find a sense of self-worth, self-satisfaction and self-fulfilment. They will also give you joy and enjoyment, meaningful happiness, a sense of energy and a sense of freedom. Do explore your intrinsic motivation but don't settle for it. Go a step further and choose to unlock your positive passion energy.

Passion and Performance

Numerous studies have shown that satisfaction with the work you do is a direct contributor to great performance and even increased profitability.[106] Given that an increased salary is no longer seen as a sustainable contribution to motivation, performance or happiness, other factors need to be considered.[107] Gallup's studies of over 17 million employees worldwide have shown the more engaged the employee is, the more customer focused and the more productive they are, and the less likely they are to leave to go to a competitor.[108] This is where passion comes in.

Passion energy is the antidote to lethargic disengagement from work. It's also the extra topping on good performance that has the power to make it great. In the famous words of Steve Jobs, "*The only way to do great work is to love what you do.*" Passion is the thing that sets you on fire in a way that gives you enthusiasm, energy,[109] liveliness,[110] vitality,[111] exuberance,[112] vigour[113] and engagement in what you do.[114] You have the power to choose to bring this positive, high energy buzz to your work.

This doesn't mean you have to be extroverted, loud and take over the place. It means that you put your heart and soul into what you do. It means that you do your work, just as you ought to live your whole life – wholeheartedly. When you choose to make passion a part of your life, including your working life, your heart will follow where the head goes. When you start to act the passionate part and succeed in it, you'll quickly discover you've become the part. The more deliberately and consciously you act with passion, the more you will feel it. It's simple: passion begets passion. Use these five passion keys to nurture it, develop it, and cultivate it.

Mark Sanborn summarises the effects of passion on your performance beautifully in *The Encore Effect*.[115] First, it invigorates you in a way that makes you jump out of bed ready to get to the important work whose purpose you understand. Secondly, it inspires you to aspire higher and see farther into the future with a hopeful vision. It also sustains you, creating a whole new type of persistence because you understand the why behind what you do. When you commit to doing things with passion, you gain a sense of comfort because regardless of the outcome you know you've tried your best. It pushes your boundaries of what's possible and encourages you to initiate as well as accept new challenges. It makes you into a finisher because you learn to commit to work that is worthwhile so you never fail to complete it because of its importance to you. Last but not least, it enhances the value and benefits of the work you do because you are doing it with your full heart.

This is highlighted in a study that looked at an individual's orientation to work.[116] You can see your role as a job, which means it is simply a source of income that you can spend elsewhere to find enjoyment. If you go a step further you can see it as a career, which is defined as a way to achieve self-esteem, status, and power. Last

214 | Susanna Halonen

but not least, if you truly want to connect with your work with passion, you see it as calling. You find doing your work intrinsically rewarding and you see it as a core part of your existence.

It's clear that a big part of bringing out your passion in the workplace is about understanding how you're doing work that matters. Sometimes people have this misconception that you need to save lives, abolish poverty or work for a charity in order to do work that matters. This couldn't be farther from the truth. Every job role in this world has a purpose behind it. You just need to understand what it is and connect with it. Somehow we have become so obsessed with a specific role's responsibilities that we have forgotten to think back to why the role was created in the first place and how it creates positive impact.

As you can see, passion is a lot more accessible than you think and it has little to do with tying it to a specific activity. You have the choice to bring it with you to the workplace and use it in everything you do. This is your opportunity to truly stand out and discover how to perform at your best. Create a meaningful connection to your work and you'll feel the passion within you flare up.

Finding the Passion in What You Do

Now it is time for you to start unravelling your meaningful connection to your work. The questions that follow will help you to explore how the five passion keys already exist in the work you do. If you're quite happy and satisfied at work, you might find it easy to answer these questions. Even if this is the case, I encourage you to think about your answers and whether you think they are bringing out your most passionate self. I want you to think of how you could go a step further to find even more passion, fulfilment and performance at work.

On the other hand, if you're not feeling very engaged or happy at work, this is your opportunity to change that. Even though your employer has the responsibility to provide you with certain resources that make it possible for you to do your work well and find happiness at work, in the end it's your responsibility to choose to be passionate, to be happy and to perform at your best in the workplace. This is your opportunity to tap into your subconscious and to think about why it is that you chose to do this work in the first place. Often, this is the key to reconnecting with your work and doing it with passion.

1. How is the work you're doing, or the company you're working for, aligned with who you are?

A big part of being able to bring out your passion in the workplace is understanding how your real self is coming out in the work you do. Think about how your values and beliefs are aligned with the work you do, and how similar they are to the values of the company you work for. Often we're naturally attracted to roles and companies that are similar to ourselves yet we rarely take the time to acknowledge that and instead run away somewhere else looking for greener grass.

Really stop to think about this. Why did you decide to do this work in the first place? What was it about the company that attracted you to it? What made you apply for the role, and accept it? Even if you can't see a clear value match between you and the company, how is it that the work you do enables you to stay true to who you are? Spend some time on this question and create a list of all the different ways your true self is connected to your work.

Becoming aware of this authentic connection with your work and understanding it is the first step to creating passion for your work. If you want to take it a step further, you can brainstorm how you could bring your authentic self more into the work you do. Could you approach existing tasks and projects in a new way that's more natural to you? Could you interact with your colleagues in a more authentic way that lets them see more of the real you (not just the 'working you')? Could you talk to your manager about what values drive you and how you could incorporate them into your role more? These are only a few ideas that some of my existing clients have put into place but it's up to you to think about what works best for you and test it out.

2. What is the positive impact you're creating with the work you do, or by being a part of this company?

This is the part where you think about the why behind what you do. What is your purpose at work and what kind of positive impact are you creating? Remember that positive impact comes in many shapes and forms, and it's about you understanding what positive impact you directly want to create. Is the work you're doing making someone else's work easier so they have less stress and are able to be more productive? Is the work you're doing driving creativity and innovation in the company, which in turn is helping the world progress?

Also think about the personal impact you are creating with all the day-to-day interactions you have with your work, be it face-to-face, through the phone, through email, or even through social media. It could be that simply your presence in a room has the power to infect more passion and positivity around you if you're in the right frame of mind. Maybe you're the one in the team with optimism and vision for the future, and you infect others with that positivity. Or perhaps you're the critical one making sure that new ideas are assessed for safety, risk and effectiveness. Get creative here and don't limit yourself. Think about all the possible ways you're having a positive effect right now.

What impact would people say your work is having on the world? What is the personal brand you carry with you, or the personal brand you would like to clearly demonstrate? How is what you're doing contributing to the awesomeness in this world?

What's the mark that you're leaving on the planet, and what are you getting known for by doing the work you do? Again, think about how you can maximise this positive impact and maybe even venture into a new type of influence. Ask yourself, what's the smallest step you could take right now that would have the biggest, most positive impact? After an interaction with someone, are you leaving them better off than how they were when you found them?

3. How is your work helping you to learn and grow as a person daily?

The next step to unlocking your passion in the workplace is to identify how your work is helping you to grow and develop. How is it helping you to reach your potential, and become the best version of you that you could possibly be? What are you doing daily that makes you move forward from who you were yesterday to who you are today? How are you enhancing your skills and developing your natural traits through your work?

This is where a sense of progress is important. When you set your goals, or are given goals to reach, break them down into smaller manageable mini goals. Think about how these mini goals could be positioned more like mastery goals rather than fixed goals. Fixed goals are the ones that are about reaching X sales or Y return on investment, whereas mastery goals are all about improving yourself and learning how to be your most effective. Setting these mini mastery goals to help you reach the fixed goals you are given by the business will naturally make you more passionate about them. You will also be more driven to achieve them because they are positioned in a way that focuses on your development.

Remember that learning isn't about attending training courses or being told how to do something. It's about taking initiative to develop yourself daily. Have conversations with your colleagues, read different articles, watch inspirational talks, have a mentor, try doing something differently, and take on challenges you have no idea how to solve. The organisation you work for has a responsibility to provide training, for sure. But again, it's your responsibility to choose to embrace your learning self daily. This is how you'll unlock your passion and make your performance soar.

4. Who are the people in your work that you connect with in a way that they form a part of your tribe?

Having friends at work is one of the key drivers of engagement in the workplace.[117] Truly connecting with colleagues in a way that they form a part of your tribe drives your passion at work. This means you bring your authentic self to work and let your colleagues see you in your wholehearted way. No, this doesn't mean you don't remain professional, it simply means that you remain real. Be honest about who you are and you'll find it easier to connect with your colleagues while encouraging them to be their real selves. That's when you'll see who the really like-minded people are, and you have the opportunity to invite them to your tribe.

Who in your work already encourages you and helps you be your best possible self? Who in your work can you have real conversations with about things unrelated to work? Who in your work supports you in your dreams and pushes you to aim high? Who in your work inspires you? Who in your work has this positive, passionate energy that gets you excited just by being in their company? Don't only think about your direct team but the people around in the environment as well as across the whole organisation. Maybe the clients or vendors you work with through your work also form a part of your passion tribe. If you're self-employed, think about the people you regularly meet up with to discuss business who light you up – be it your clients, mentors or other entrepreneurs.

Stop the detrimental 'eating lunch by your desk' culture that exists in so many organisations today. Take 30 minutes out of the office to have real conversations with your colleagues and clients. You will connect with each other better, inspire each other to be your best selves, and help each other to unlock your passions. Be yourself at work and you'll find it easier to find like-minded people to connect with. Together, you can light each other up and create a passion ripple effect across the workplace you're in.

5. How do you use your natural strengths in a variety of ways in your work daily?

Investigating how you are already using your natural, positive traits in your work will give you that final push to unlocking your passion fully. You are probably already using your strengths in the work you do without being fully aware of it. The more aware you become of putting your natural abilities to use in the work you do, the more you will be able to enjoy them, make the most of them, and use them more in different ways. This is the bulletproof way of going from engagement to enjoyment to passion at work. These in turn will boost your performance in what you do.

Remember that it's counterproductive (and no fun) to focus on your weaknesses when you have all these amazing, unique strengths you can use. Really focus on how you can put them to use in a varied way through your working day and week. Using them in new ways daily will improve your creativity, avoid their overuse, and even contribute to improving some of your weaknesses that are detrimental to your work.

Think about the five prominent strengths you identified in yourself in the previous chapter. How are you using them in your work right now? When do they usually shine the most? How are they making you enjoy your job more? How are they helping you to perform? In what different ways, or in what different situations, are you putting them to use right now? The key here is to think of how you can vary their use in a way that helps you create maximum positive impact while helping you grow. Good at communication? Can you do more work that enables you to write or design reports that communicate effectively? Or maybe you can work at using your communication to present important ideas to your team or the wider company? Or maybe you could even help others to communicate better? The opportunities to try different things are endless.

Also stay open minded to the strengths you have. If you think one (or some) of them don't fit in the workplace, think again. One of my clients once said to me, *"Yes but my strength is kindness. What good is that in the workplace?"* The answer is it's good in an infinite number of ways! It helps you have better relationships with your colleagues, clients and suppliers. It helps you be more understanding of constructive feedback because you see it as a kindness from your manager as they simply want to help you improve. It can help you deliver bad news in a kinder way. And the list goes on. Every strength has its unique benefits in unique situations. You simply have to think out of the box here and identify its benefits for the situations you're in. It's all about positioning. Now ask yourself, how could you be using your strengths in different ways across your working day?

Your Turn to Tap into Your Inner Passion at Work
Now it's time you moved this passion from reflection to action. Become more aware of how the work you do is aligned with who you are and the positive impact you're creating. Make an effort to learn and grow daily at your work, connect with the tribe connected with your work, and put your natural strengths to good use in different ways. Start small and you'll see these things becoming more natural to you. The more natural they become, the more you'll feel that positive passion energy within you burn strong. Go and connect with your work wholeheartedly, and let that passion of yours come out in its full vigour.

Passion is born when you catch a glimpse of your true potential.
~ Zig Ziglar ~

nine

Ready to Unlock Your Passion?

There is no passion to be found playing small – in settling
for a life that is less than the one you are capable of living.
~ *Nelson Mandela* ~

Passion, just like happiness, is natural to life and to you because it is a part of the self. We now know passion isn't reserved for the lucky few who choose to commit their lives to one activity or thing. It is available to you and to everyone throughout life. It exists in you and in everyone in infinitely flexible forms. It's your perception of reality that makes it possible for you to awaken it and unlock it.

Learn to know yourself and you will access passion at its source. Become more aware of your authentic self and you will bring that fire inside of you alive. Accept yourself for who you are and understand how the choices you make daily are tied to that. Choose to see the passion in yourself, and believe in it, and you will not have any outwards obstacles to being passionate. The inner and outer worlds are mirrors of each other, and hence the more you connect with your passion, the easier you'll find it to be passionate across your life. That way you will make passion a habit. You will discover a passionate way of being.

This passionate way of being doesn't only connect you with your heart but also runs throughout your whole body fuelling your energy and drive. It powers your mind and body in a way that connects you with the wonder, joy and playfulness of a child. It helps you to embrace the spontaneity of life, and manifest passion in a way that it enhances your life. It has the power to help you find momentary joy, meaningful happiness, and lifelong fulfilment. It has the power to help you find love in what you do.

Being Passionate

Instead of limiting your passion to an activity, this is your opportunity to see passion as something that can be implemented and expressed across your life. In fact, it is this variety of pursuing different things passionately that plays a role in feeding the passion. By getting in touch with your authentic self and understanding your why it's less likely you will get stuck on one specific activity for life. This idea of being passionate across your life acknowledges and embraces your dynamic identity that is continuously evolving.[118] It makes it possible for you to take passion with you throughout your life wherever you go.

Having awareness of your dynamic identity and using it to remain passionate makes it possible for you to have long-term happiness and fulfilment. This is a more holistic approach to achieving meaningful happiness and outweighs the benefits of temporary positive emotions you would get from tying your passion to one activity obsessively. This approach to passion recognises how finding love and enjoyment across your life further reinforces the passion in itself. This is your opportunity to choose passion on a daily basis in order to enhance your life and help you create a life worth living.

The Passion Keys
Some people spend their whole lives looking for passion when in fact it's right in front of their eyes. It's inside of them and they can choose to bring it out at any time by connecting with the five passion keys. Being passionate isn't about finding an activity or thing to tie your passion to, but unlocking it from within you. Here is a reminder of the five passion keys and how they bring out your positive passion energy.

1. **Be the authentic you.**
   Discover what your current values and beliefs are, and how you are using them in your daily life. This will help you create a meaningful connection to everything you do as you understand how your different activities enable you to connect with your true self. Shift your idea of authenticity from your self-image to your true self, and you will find passion that no one can take away from you.

2. **Understand your why.**

   Think about the positive impact you want to create and the why behind what you do. When you understand the purpose behind your actions and how they are positively influencing the world in its own way, you will feel passionate about what you do.

3. **Master the art of learning.**

   Embrace your most driven learning self and see every day as an exciting opportunity to grow and develop. Be adventurous with how you develop your self and always aim for mastering who you are. Be your best possible self and you will be your most passionate self.

4. **Connect with your tribe.**

   Spend time with the people who inspire, encourage and motivate you. Find people you look up to who get your positive energy fired up. Connect with these people and ignite each others' fires.

5. **Play with your strengths.**

   Understand your positive natural traits and the power they have when you put them to good use in different ways. Embody them in your everyday and vary how, when, and where you use them to have fun with them. Let them drive you to your most passionate, best performing self.

Act Out Passion

As I've outlined in this book, the secret to building a fulfilling life full of passion isn't to chase passion but to proactively bring it out yourself. In the empty spaces below, I want you to commit to five actions you are going to take in the next month so you can start to embrace your passionate way of being and live a life full of positive passion energy. I want you to commit to five actions to start with so you avoid overwhelm and begin to discover what it is like to be passionate. This book is a useful start in helping you to reflect and understand how to bring out your passion, but it is only through action that you can make it happen. Test different things and see what works for you. Remain self-aware and go with your intuition on what you think brings out your passion the most.

Because there are five keys that connect you to your passion, unlock it, and reinforce the passion energy cycle, I would recommend you choose one action from each of the five elements to create a sustainable passion energy within you. Goals and actions that are written down and have a date and time make it easier for you to stick to them. In order to maximise your likelihood of successfully unlocking your passion, write down the specific actions you are going to take, and when you are going to take them, below.

1. Your action for enhancing your connection to your authentic self:

Date you will do it:

2. Your action for connecting with your why and the positive impact you want to create:

Date you will do it:

3. Your action for embracing your learning self:

Date you will do it:

4. Your action for interacting with your tribe:

Date you will do it:

5. Your action for using your strengths in different ways:

Date you will do it:

Once you've completed these actions, it's up to you to add new ones that keep the passion energy alive. The more you do these kinds of actions, the more natural it will become and the sooner you'll be able to embrace being passionate across your life as a habit.

Choose Passion Everyday
You can choose how to think, feel and act. Your choice affects how you experience things. This means you can choose to be passionate and live your whole life with passion. This means that passion can be a type of positive energy that exists across your life. If you choose it

to be so. And that's my message to you. Don't settle for a life without passion. Think big and aim high. Learn to unlock the passion within you, and you'll discover your passion creating even more passion. Make being passionate a habit and use it to live an extraordinarily fulfilling life.

Break free from the one-passion myth and embrace your whole life passionately.
~ Susanna Halonen ~

APPENDICES

Cheat Sheet

Some of the exercises that you do when you are learning how to connect with your passion keys ask you to create lists or give lots of options. In order to really make the most of these exercises, try to stay with them until you feel yourself struggle. It's when you struggle that you are at the brink of discovering something meaningful so take discomfort as a sign that you need to keep going.

Here are some questions that can help you create more lists, think creatively, and tap into your subconscious:

- What else?
- Think of one more idea.
- Think of three more ideas.
- If you had all the time in the world, what would you do?
- If you had all the money in the world, what would you do?
- If you could do anything, what would you do? If you can't do that, what's the next best thing you could do?
- If you had to help a friend to complete this list, what would you recommend for them to add?

Notes

Introduction
[1] Achor, S. (2010). *The Happiness Advantage: The Seven Principles of Positive Psychology that Fuel Success and Performance at Work.* New York, NY: Crown Business.
[2] Halonen, S. & Lomas, T. (2014). A passionate way of being: A qualitative study revealing the passion spiral. *International Journal of Psychological Research, 7(2),* 17-28.

Chapter One: Exploring Passion
[3] Merriam Webster (26 Aug 2014). Search dictionary for 'passion'. Retrieved from: http://www.merriam-webster.com/dictionary/passion
[4] Waterman, A. S. (1993). Two conceptions of happiness: Contrasts of personal expressiveness (eudaimonia) and hedonic enjoyment. *Journal of Personality and Social Psychology, 64(4),* 678–691.
[5] Ryan, R. M. & Deci, E. L. (2001). On happiness and human potentials: A review of research on hedonic and eudaimonic wellbeing. *Annual Review of Psychology, 52(1),* 141–166.
[6] Rony, J. A. (1990). *Les Passions.* Paris: Presses Universitaires de France.

[7] Rony, J. A. (1990). *Les Passions*. Paris: Presses Universitaires de France.

[8] Vallerand, R. J., & Verner-Filion, J. (2013). Making people's life most worth living: On the importance of passion for positive psychology. *Terapia Psicologica, 31*(1), 35–48.

[9] Gamsu, M. (2010). Passion and Detachment: Kierkegaard's Knight of Faith. *Existential Analysis, 21*(1), 63–75.

[10] Author Unknown (*Year Unknown*). Kierkegaard & Nietzsche: Two Different Passions. Retrieved from: http://www.sorenkierkegaard.nl/artikelen/Engels/036.%20Kierkegaardand%20Nietzsche%20 2%20different%20passions.pdf

[11] Vallerand, R. J., Blanchard, C., Mageau, G. A., Koestner, R., Ratelle, C., Leonard, M. & Gagne, M. (2003). Les Passions de l'Ame: On obsessive and harmonious passion. *Journal of Personality and Social Psychology, 85*(4), 756–767.

[12] Vallerand, R. J., Blanchard, C., Mageau, G. A., Koestner, R., Ratelle, C., Leonard, M. & Gagne, M. (2003). Les Passion de l'Ame: On obsessive and harmonious passion. *Journal of Personality and Social Psychology, 85*(4), 756–767.

[13] Vallerand, R. J., & Verner-Filion, J. (2013). Making people's life most worth living: On the importance of passion for positive psychology. *Terapia Psicologica, 31*(1), 35–48.

[14] Amiot, C. E., Vallerand, R. J., & Blanchard, C. M. (2006). Passion and psychological adjustment: A test

of the person-environment fit hypothesis. *Personality and Social Psychology Bulletin, 32*(2), 220–229.

[15] TED.com (26 Aug 2014). Technology, Entertainment and Design: Ideas Worth Spreading. Retrieved from: http://www.ted.com/

[16] Halonen, S. & Lomas, T. (2014). A passionate way of being: A qualitative study revealing the passion spiral. *International Journal of Psychological Research, 7(2),* 17-28.

Chapter Two: Why is Passion Important

[17] Vallerand, R. J. (2008). On the psychology of passion: In search of what makes people's lives most worth living. *Canadian Psychologist, 49*(1), 1–13.

[18] Hefferon, K. & Boniwell, I. (2011). *Positive Psychology: Theory, Research and Applications [Kindle version].* New York, NY: Open University Press.

[19] Ryan, R. M. & Deci, E. L. (2001). On happiness and human potentials: A review of research on hedonic and eudaimonic wellbeing. *Annual Review of Psychology, 52*(1), 141–166.

[20] Halonen, S. & Lomas, T. (2014). A passionate way of being: A qualitative study revealing the passion spiral. *International Journal of Psychological Research, 7(2),* 17-28.

[21] Halonen, S. & Lomas, T. (2014). A passionate way of being: A qualitative study revealing the passion spiral. *International Journal of Psychological Research, 7(2),* 17-28.

[22] Baumeister, R. F., Bratslavsky, E., Finkenauer, C., & Vohs, K. D. (2001). Bad is stronger than good. *Review of General Psychology, 5*(4), 323–370.

[23] Achor, S. (2010). *The Happiness Advantage: The Seven Principles of Positive Psychology that Fuel Success and Performance at Work.* New York, NY: Crown Business.

[24] Fredrickson, B. L. (1998). What good are positive emotions? *Review of General Psychology, 2*(3), 300–319; Fredrickson, B. L. (2001). The role of positive emotions in positive psychology: The broaden-and-build theory of positive emotions. *American Psychologist, 56*(3), 218–226.

[25] Estrada, C. A., Isen, A. M., & Young, M.J. (1997). Positive affect facilitates integration of information and decreases anchoring in reasoning among physicians. *Organizational and Human Decision Processes, 72*(1), 117–135; Estrada, C., Isen, A. M., & Young, M. J. (1994). Positive affect influences creative problem solving and reported source of practice satisfaction in physicians. *Motivation and Emotion, 18*(4), 285–299

[26] Vallerand, R. J. (2008). On the psychology of passion: In search of what makes people's lives most worth living. *Canadian Psychologist, 49*(1), 1–13.

[27] Achor, S. (2013). *Before Happiness: Five Actionable Strategies to Create a Positive Path to Success.* New York: The Random House Group.

[28] Vallerand, R. J. (2008). On the psychology of passion: In search of what makes people's lives most worth living. *Canadian Psychologist, 49*(1), 1–13.

[29] Rip, B., Fortin, S., & Vallerand, R. J. (2006). The relationship between passion and injury in dance students. *Journal of Dance Medicine & Science, 10*(1–2), 14–20.

[30] Finkelstein, S. R., and Fishbach, A. (2012). Tell me what I did wrong: Experts seek and respond to negative feedback. *Journal of Consumer Research, 39*(1), 22–38.

Chapter Three: Be the Authentic You

[31] Style, C. (2011). *Brilliant Positive Psychology: What makes us happy, optimistic and motivated.* Harlow: Pearson Education Limited.

[32] Crabtree, S. (8 Oct 2013). Worldwide, 13% Employees are Engaged at Work. *Gallup World.* Retrieved from: http://www.gallup.com/poll/165269/worldwide-employees-engaged-work.aspx

[33] Style, C. (2011). *Brilliant Positive Psychology: What makes us happy, optimistic and motivated.* Harlow: Pearson Education Limited.

[34] Ryan, R. M. & Deci, E. L. (2001). On happiness and human potentials: A review of research on hedonic and eudaimonic wellbeing. *Annual Review of Psychology, 52*(1), 141–166.

[35] Sagiv, L., Roccas, S., & Hazan, O. (2004). Value pathways to well-being: Healthy values, valued goal attainment and environmental congruence. In P. A. Linley and S. Joseph (eds.), *Positive Psychology in Practice.* Hoboken, NJ: John Wiley and Sons, pp.68–84.

[36] Waterman, A. S. (1990). Personal expressiveness: Philosophical and psychological foundations. *Journal of Mind and Behaviour, 11*(1), 47–74.

[37] Sagiv, L., Roccas, S., and Hazan, O. (2004). Value pathways to well-being: Healthy values, valued goal attainment and environmental congruence. In P.A Linley and S. Joseph (eds.), *Positive Psychology in Practice*. Hoboken, NJ: John Wiley and Sons, pp. 68–84.

[38] Ryan, R. M., and Deci, E. L. (2000). Self-determination theory and the facilitation of intrinsic motivation, social development, and well-being. *American Psychologist, 55*(1), 68–78.

[39] Waterman, A. S. (1990). Personal expressiveness: Philosophical and psychological foundations. *Journal of Mind and Behaviour, 11*(1), 47–74.

[40] Deci, E. I. and Ryan, R. M. (2000). The "What" and "Why" of goal pursuits: Human needs and the self-determination of behavior. *Psychological Inquiry, 11*(4), 227–268.

[41] TED.com (Jun 2010). Talk titled *"The power of vulnerability"* by B. Brown. Retrieved from: https://www.ted.com/talks/brene_brown_on_vulnerability

[42] Brown, B. (2013). *Daring Greatly: How the Courage to Be Vulnerable Transforms the Way we Live, Love, Parent and Lead*. New York: Penguin Group (USA).

[43] Goleman, D. (1996). *Emotional Intelligence: Why It Can Matter More than IQ*. London: Bloomsbury Publishing.

[44] Gilbert, D. (2007). *Stumbling on Happiness*. New York: Random House, Inc.

[45] *The Legend of Bagger Vance* (2000). [Film] Directed by Robert Redford, screenplay by Jeremy Leven. USA: Dreamworks Pictures/20th Century Fox.

Chapter Four: Find Your Why

[46] Harter, S. (2005). Authenticity. In C. R. Snyder and S. J. Lopez (eds), *Handbook of Positive Psychology*. Oxford: Oxford University Press, p.390.

[47] Gallup, Inc. (26 May 1999). Item 10: I have a best friend at work. *Gallup Business Journal*. Retrieved from: http://businessjournal.gallup.com/content/511/item-10-best-friend-work.aspx

[48] Nelson, S. K., Kushlev, K., English, T., Dunn, E. W., & Lyubomirsky, S. (2012). In defence of parenthood: Children are associated with more joy than misery. *Psychological Science, 24*(1), 3–10.

[49] Tanenhaus, S. (15 Aug 2014). Generation Nice: The Millennials are generation nice. *New York Times* Online. Retrieved from: http://www.nytimes.com/2014/08/17/fashion/the-millennials-are-generation-nice.html?_r=0

[50] Gallup (10 May 1999). Item 8: My Company's Mission or Purpose. *Gallup Business Journal Online*. Retrieved from: http://businessjournal.gallup.com/content/505/item-8-my-companys-mission-or-purpose.aspx

[51] Compton, W. C., Smith, M. L., Cornish, K. A. & Qualls, D. L. (1996). Factor structure of mental health measures. *Journal of Personality and Social Psychology, 71*(2), 406–413.

[52] Baumeister, R. F., & Vohs, K. D. (2005). Meaningfulness in life. In C. R. Snyder and S. J. Lopez (eds.), *Handbook of Positive Psychology*. Oxford: Oxford University Press, p.614.

[53] Baumeister, R. F., and Vohs, K. D. (2005). Meaningfulness in life. In C. R. Snyder and S. J. Lopez

(eds), *Handbook of Positive Psychology.* Oxford: Oxford University Press, p. 614.

54 Boyle, P. A., Buchman, A. S., Barnes, L. L., & Bennett, D. A. (2010). Effect of a purpose in life on risk of incident Alzheimer disease and mild cognitive impairment in community-dwelling older persons. *Archives of General Psychiatry, 67*(3), 304–10.

55 Boniwell, I., and Zimbardo, P. Balancing time perspective in pursuit of optimal functioning. In: P. A. Linley and S. Joseph (eds.). *Positive Psychology in Practice.* John Wiley & Sons; New Jersey: 2004, pp.165–178.

56 Sinek, S. (2011). *Start with Why: How Great Leaders Inspire Everyone to Take Action.* London: Penguin Group.

57 Ciraldo, J. C. (20 Sep 2012). Rational Mind vs. Emotional Mind. Retrieved from: http://www.personal. psu.edu/afr3/blogs/siowfa12/2012/09/rational-mind-vs-emotional-mind.html

58 Flora, C. (01 May 2007). Gut Almighty: Intuition really does come from the gut. *Psychology Today Online.* Retrieved from: http://www.psychologytoday.com/articles/200704/gut-almighty

59 Achor, S. (2013). *Before Happiness: Five Actionable Strategies to Create a Positive Path to Success.* New York: The Random House Group.

60 Layous, K., Nelson, S. K., and Lyubomirsky, S. (2013). What is the optimal way to deliver a positive activity intervention? The case of writing about one's best possible selves. *Journal of Happiness Studies, 14*(2), 635–654.

Chapter Five: Master the Art of Learning

[61] Dweck, C. (2006). *Mindset: The New Psychology of Success.* New York: Random House, Inc.

[62] Doidge, N. (2007). *The Brain that Changes Itself.* New York: Penguin;

Schwartz, J. M. & Begley, S. (2003). *The Mind and the Brain: Neuroplasticity and the Power of Mental Force.* New York: Harper Perennial.

[63] Fredrickson, B. L., & Branigan, C. (2005). Positive emotions broaden the scope of attention and thought-action repertoires. *Cognition and Emotion, 19*(3), 313–332.

[64] Hughes, T. F., Chang, C. C., Bilt, J. V., & Ganguli, M. (2010). Engagement in reading and hobbies and risk of incident dementia: The MoVIEWS Project. *Am J Alzheimers Dis Other Demen,* 25(5), 432–438;

Wilson, R. S., Scherr, P. A., Schneider, J. A., Tang, Y., & Bennett, D. A. (2007). Relation of cognitive activity to risk of developing Alzheimer disease. *Neurology, 69*(20), 1911–1920.

[65] Hughes, T. F., Chang, C. C., Bilt, J. V., & Ganguli, M. (2010). Engagement in reading and hobbies and risk of incident dementia: The MoVIEWS Project. *Am J Alzheimers Dis Other Demen,* 25(5), 432–438;

Wilson, R. S., Scherr, P. A., Schneider, J. A., Tang, Y., & Bennett, D. A. (2007). Relation of cognitive activity to risk of developing Alzheimer disease. *Neurology, 69*(20), 1911–1920.

[66] Zimmermann, Manfred (1986). Neurophysiology of Sensory Systems, in Robert F. Schmidt (ed.), *Fundamental of Sensory Physiology.* Springer: New York: p.116.

[67] Dweck, C. (2006). *Mindset: The New Psychology of Success.* New York: Random House, Inc.

[68] Dweck, C. (2006). *Mindset: The New Psychology of Success.* New York: Random House, Inc.

[69] Csikszentmihalyi, M. (1990). *Flow: The Psychology of Optimal Experience.* New York: Harper & Row.

Chapter Six: Connect with Your Tribe

[70] Baumeister, R. F. and Leary, M. R. (1995). The need to belong: Desire for interpersonal attachments as a fundamental human motivation. *Psychological Bulletin, 117*(3), 497–529.

[71] Thomas, Ben (6 Nov 2012). What's so special about mirror neurons? *Scientific American Blog.* Retrieved from: http://blogs.scientificamerican.com/guest-blog/2012/11/06/whats-so-special-about-mirror-neurons/

[72] The Soul Connection Network (2014). The New Psychology Part 2: Mirror Neurons. Retrieved from: http://soulconnection.net/mirror_neurons.html

[73] Winerman, Lea (2005). The mind's mirror. *Monitor on Psychology: American Psychological Association, 36*(9), 48. Retrieved from: http://www.apa.org/monitor/oct05/mirror.aspx

[74] Marsh, Jason (29 Mar 2012). Do mirror neurons give us empathy? *Greater Good: The Science of a Meaningful Life.* Retrieved from: http://greatergood.berkeley.edu/article/item/do_mirror_neurons_give_empathy

[75] Barsade, S. G. (2002). The ripple effect: Emotional contagion and its influence on group behavior. *Administrative Science Quarterly, 47*(4), 644–675.

[76] Sy, T., Côté, S., & Saavedra, R. (2005). The contagious leader: Impact of the leader's mood on the mood of group members, group affective tone, and group processes. *Journal of Applied Psychology, 90*(2), 295.

[77] Deci, E. I. and Ryan, R. M. (2000). The "What" and "Why" of goal pursuits: Human needs and the self-determination of behavior. *Psychological Inquiry, 11*(4), 227–268.

Marcus Aurelius (1997). *Meditations.* Ware, Herts: Wordsworth Editions, p.54

[78] TED.com (Dec 2013). Talk titled *"Never, ever give up"* by Diana Nyad. Retrieved from: http://www.ted.com/talks/diana_nyad_never_ever_give_up

[79] School of Life (Event on 4 May 2014). Titled *"In Conversation with Arianna Huffington"*. More information retrievable from: http://www.theschooloflife.com/shop/in-conversation-with-arianna-huffington/

[80] Huffington, A. (2014). *Thrive: The Third Metric to Redefining Success and Creating a Happier Life.* Published by The Random House Group Limited.

[81] TED.com (Feb 2012). Talk titled "Connected, but alone?" by Sherry Turkle. Retrieved from: http://www.ted.com/talks/sherry_turkle_alone_together

[82] Trenholm, Rich (7 Mar 2013). You spend 23 days a year on your phone, say new figures. *CNET.* Retrieved from: http://www.cnet.com/uk/news/you-spend-23-days-a-year-on-your-phone-say-new-figures/ Woollaston, Victoria (8 Oct 2013). How often do you check your phone? The average person does it 110 times a DAY. *MailOnline.* Retrieved from: http://www.

dailymail.co.uk/sciencetech/article-2449632/How-check-phone-The-average-person-does-110-times-DAY-6-seconds-evening.html

[83] Hobbs, Nicola Jane (1 Feb 2014). 5 Reasons to turn your phone off (now!). *MindBodyGreen.* Retrieved from: http://www.mindbodygreen.com/0-12420/5-reasons-to-turn-your-phone-off-now.html

[84] Lyubomirsky, S. R. and Ross, L. (1997). Hedonic consequences of social comparison: A contrast of happy and unhappy people. *Journal of Personality and Social Psychology, 73*(6), 1141–57.

[85] Lyubomirsky, S., Tucker, K. L. and Kasri, R. (2001). Responses to hedonically conflicting social comparisons: Comparing happy and unhappy individuals. *European Journal of Social Psychology, 31*(5), 511–535.

Chapter Seven: Play with Your Strengths

[86] Seligman, M. E. Pl, Steen, T., Park, N., & Peterson, C. (2005). Positive psychology progress: Empirical validation of interventions. *American Psychologist, 60*(5), 410–21.

[87] Harzer, C., & Ruch, W. (2012). The application of signature character strengths and positive experiences at work. *Journal of Happiness Studies, 6,* 1–19;

Littman-Ovadia, H., & Davidovitch, N. (2010). Effects of congruence and character-strength deployment on work adjustment and well-being. *International Journal of Business and Social Science, 1*(3), 138–146;

Littman-Ovadia, H., & Steger, M. (2010). Character strengths and well-being among volunteers and employees. Toward an integrative model. *Journal of Positive Psychology, 5*(6), 419–430.

[88] Crabb, S. (2011). The use of coaching principles to foster employee engagement. *The Coaching Psychologist, 7*(1), 27–34.

[89] Asplund, J. (2012, September 27). When Americans Use Their Strengths More, They Stress Less. *Gallup Wellbeing.* Retrieved from http://www.gallup.com/poll/157679/americans-strengths-stress-less.aspx

[90] Asplund, J. (2012, September 27). When Americans Use Their Strengths More, They Stress Less. *Gallup Wellbeing Online.* Retrieved from http://www.gallup.com/poll/157679/americans-strengths-stress-less.aspx

[91] Grandey, A. A., Fiske, G. M., Mattila, A. S., Jansen, K. J. & Sideman, L. A. (2005). Is "service with a smile" enough? Authenticity of positive displays during service encounters. *Organisational Behaviour and Human Decision Processes, 96*(1), 38–55;

Kahn, W. A. (1990). Psychological conditions of personal engagement and disengagement at work. *Academy of Management Journal, 33*(4), 692–724.

[92] Ryan, R. M., & Deci, E. L. (2002). Overview of self-determination theory: An organismic dialectical perspective. In R. M. Ryan & E. L. Deci (Eds.), *Handbook of Self-Determination Research.* Rochester, NY: The University of Rochester Press.

[93] Elston, F. & Boniwell, I. (2011). A grounded theory study of the value derived by women in financial services through coaching intervention to help them identify their strengths and practise using them in the workplace. *International Coaching Psychology Review, 6*(1), 16–32.

[94] Linley, P. A., & Harrington, S. (2006). Strengths coaching: A potential-guided approach to coaching psychology. *International Coaching Psychology Review, 1*(1), 37–46.

[95] Linley, A., Nielsen, K. M., Wood, A. M., Gillett, R., and Biswas-Diener, R. (2010). Using signature strengths in the pursuit of goals: Effects on goal progress, need satisfaction, and well-being, and implications for coaching psychologists. *International Coaching Psychology Review, 5*(1), 6–15.

[96] Asplund, J. (2012, September 27). When Americans Use Their Strengths More, They Stress Less. *Gallup Wellbeing Online*. Retrieved from http://www.gallup.com/poll/157679/americans-strengths-stress-less.aspx

[97] VIA Institute on Character (26 Aug 2014). Applying your character strengths. Retrieved from: http://via.spotlets.com/apply

[98] Seligman, M. E. P., Park, N. & C., Peterson (2004). The Values In Action (VIA) classification of character strengths. *Ricerche di Psicologia, 27*(1), 63–78.

[99] Seligman, M. E. P., Park, N. & C., Peterson (2004). The Values In Action (VIA) classification of character strengths. *Ricerche di Psicologia, 27*(1), 63–78.

[100] VIA Institute on Character (2014). Get your free VIA Me! Character Strengths Profile. Retrieved from https://www.viame.org/survey/

[101] Centre for Applied Positive Psychology (CAPP) (26 Aug 2014). *Realise2*. Retrieved from: http://www.cappeu.com/realise2.aspx

[102] Rath, T. (2007). *Strengthsfinder 2.0*. New York: Gallup Press.

[103] TEDx Talks (11 Mar 2014). Talk titled *"The secret to living a life with passion"* by S. Halonen. Retrieved from: https://www.youtube.com/watch?v=_R236_kTYTs

Chapter Eight: Spread Passion at Work

[104] Ryan, R. M., and Deci, E. L. (2000). Self-determination theory and the facilitation of intrinsic motivation, social development, and well-being. *American Psychologist, 55*(1), 68–78.

[105] Pink, D. H. (2011). *Drive: The Surprising Truth About What Motivates Us.* New York: Canongate Books; TED.com (July 2009). Talk titled *"The puzzle of motivation"* by Dan Pink. Retrieved from: http://www.ted.com/talks/dan_pink_on_motivation?language=en

[106] Heslin, P. A. (2005). Conceptualizing and evaluating career success. *Journal of Organizational Behavior, 26*(2), 113–136.

[107] Diener, E., & Seligman, M. E. P. (2004). Beyond money: Toward an economy of well-being. *Psychological Science in the Public Interest, 5*(1), 1–31.

[108] On page 105 in Greenberg, M., & Maymin, S. (2013). *Profit from the Positive: Proven Leadership Strategies to Boost Productivity and Transform Your Business.* Published by McGraw-Hill.

[109] Thayer, R. E. (1996). The origin of everyday moods: Managing energy, tension and stress. New York: Oxford University Press.

[110] McNair, D. M., Lorr, M., & Droppleman, L. F. (1971). Manual for the profile of mood states. San Diego, CA: Educational and Industrial Testing Services.

[111] Ryan, R. M., & Frederick, C. (1997). On energy, personality, and health: Subjective vitality as a dynamic reflection of well-being. *Journal of Personality, 65*(3), 529–565.

[112] Jamison, K. R. (2004). *Exuberance: The passion for life.* New York: Knopf.

[113] Shirom, A. (2003). Feeling vigorous at work? The construct of vigor and the study of positive affect in organizations. In D. Ganster, & P. L. Perrewe (Eds.), *Research in organizational stress and well-being* (Vol.3, pp. 135–165). Greenwich, CT: JAI Press.

[114] Britt, T. W., Adler, A. B., & Bartone, P. T. (2001). Deriving benefits from stressful events: The role of engagement in meaningful work and hardiness. *Journal of Occupational Health Psychology, 6*(1), 53–63.

[115] Sanborn, M. (2008). *The Encore Effect.* New York: Doubleday.

[116] Bellah, R. N., Madsen, R., Sullivan, W. M., Swidler, A., & Tipton, S. M. (1985). *Habits of the heart.* New York: Harper & Row.

[117] Gallup, Inc. (26 May 1999). Item 10: I have a best friend at work. *Gallup Business Journal Online.* Retrieved from: http://businessjournal.gallup.com/content/511/item-10-best-friend-work.aspx

Chapter Nine: Ready to Unlock Your Passion

[118] Schlenker, B. R. (1985). Identity and self-identification. In B. R. Schlenker (ed.), *The self and social life* (pp. 65–99). New York: McGraw-Hill.

Made in the USA
Charleston, SC
07 April 2015